AN UNNAMED PRESS/RARE BIRD JOINT PRODUCTION

unnamedpress.com
rarebirdbooks.com

Hardcover ISBN: 978-1-961884-11-3
Ebook ISBN: 978-1-961884-12-0
Library of Congress Control Number: 2023945447

Cover painting by David Pagani
Jacket design and typeset by Jaya Nicely

Manufactured in the United States of America by Sheridan.

Distributed by Publishers Group West

First Hardcover Edition

2 4 6 8 10 9 7 5 3 1

:10 SECONDS TO AIR
MY LIFE IN THE DIRECTOR'S CHAIR

DON MISCHER

With Sara Lukinson

LOS ANGELES, CA

To Suzan

Your patience with my ups and downs in writing this book have been remarkable. On top of that, you have been my guide, keeping me on track and focused, even when I felt I was lost in the wilderness. You mean the world to me.

"In the course of my day as a director,
I'm both a tyrant and troublemaker,
visionary and a hack, therapist and provocateur
not to mention artist, basket case, and lunatic.
But in the end, I have to be the last one standing…
because I'm the director."

The Director's Creed

TABLE OF CONTENTS

:10 SECONDS TO AIR

MY LIFE IN THE DIRECTOR'S CHAIR

INTRODUCTION

People often ask me, "How did you ever end up as a producer and director of some of television's most spectacular and historic events? What was it like? Why did you put yourself in such stressful situations? What happens when things go wrong?" And my favorite, "Aren't there easier ways to earn a living?" For me it was simple. I love television. And I love making shows, working with creative people, experiencing their passion, helping them realize their dreams while facing huge challenges. Most of all, I love surprising audiences, bringing them together, and deeply moving viewers emotionally.

:10 Seconds to Air is a personal look behind the curtain at some of television's most celebrated events, from someone who has lived and worked in the thick of it for decades. It's an unlikely journey, but a very American one. It's my homage to America's vibrant, richly diverse culture, as reflected through television and witnessed by me from the catbird's seat—the director's chair. What follows are stories about high profile television events I had the opportunity to produce and direct, and about my own American journey, from being raised in a blue-collar middle-class family in a racist city in South Texas in the 1940s and '50s—to the beating heart of America's greatness. Along the way are my experiences with artists of every stripe, from whom I learned and shared the high wire act of live television.

Yes, I fell in love with live television from the get-go when I first saw it at the age of nine. I soon realized that live television came with intense pressure. Adrenaline pumping. Exhilarating. Not for the faint of heart. A job that always demands total focus, a stress level that can be scary but is so thrillingly alive, it becomes addictive. I often feel that if I don't stress about each show that I do, I won't be doing my job well. Even when producing the Spring Variety Show at Berkeley Hall Junior high school where my daughter Lilly was in the eighth grade.

I feel the tightening anxiety of stress within, but what I didn't realize until I saw the NBC news coverage of our control room at the Opening Ceremonies of the Atlanta Olympic Games, was that the stress came out in facial tics in my eyes, and twitches in my neck and shoulders—not the most attractive things to see in yourself or for others to see in a director who is trying to hold things together. It was really uncomfortable watching myself on camera directing. I actually felt sorry myself. "That poor guy! Look at that! Why does he put himself through that? Is it worth it?" The truth is, I would say yes, it is worth it. Because there is still nothing more exciting than sitting in the director's chair and counting down the seconds to the Opening Ceremonies of the Olympic Games: 10, 9, 8, 7...knowing that you'll be sharing everything you have dreamed and worked towards with eighty percent of the planet. You've spent three years on the concepts, narrative, choreography, music, costumes, and staging. You have a cast of eight thousand and volunteers numbering twenty-five hundred, not to mention eleven thousand athletes on the field.

You have only one shot to pull it off. There are no retakes. No fixes. No editing. Watching it will be a huge stadium of people, heads of state, the world press, and nearly every pair of eyes in the world. It's over in a flash. There can be agony or ecstasy. Sometimes at the same time. Many times, when I'm in this situation, I ask myself, "Can you think of a worse place to fall on your face and louse things up?"

MASTER CONTROL

I've spent a large part of my professional life inside a television production truck or in a massive and darkened control room. Both are kind of a cocoon of chaos from which you try to spin a story. All you see are television screens—everywhere. They become your eyes to the world. Cameras—sometimes as many as thirty-five to forty—are planted in some of the most unlikely places, like Argus Panoptes, the many-eyed giant of Greek mythology. It's where we get the expression, "the eyes of Argus follow you."

So, imagine you are in the master control room. The tension builds as you are counting down to a major live broadcast. Dozens of headset channels are buzzing with last minute updates and stand-bys as you approach the final second to going on the air. Lighting cues are triggered, horns go up in the orchestra, the talent are set on their opening marks, cameras are being readied for their opening moves. It's a frantic level of intense activity—overwhelmingly exciting, full of anticipation and some apprehension, expectancy, and sometimes pure joy. Suddenly, the associate director shouts, "10 seconds to air...9...8...7!"

All at once, there's an eerie quiet. You take a deep breath and buckle your seatbelt as you begin to call the shots at a nonstop pace for the next few hours, which you know will be a wild rollercoaster ride.

This has been my life for the last six decades—creating, producing, and directing some of the most celebrated televised events—from the Opening and Closing Ceremonies of both the Summer and Winter Olympic Games to *Carnegie Hall: Live at 100*; from Super Bowl halftime shows with Michael Jackson, Bruce Springsteen, Paul McCartney, the Rolling Stones, and Prince, to the Kennedy Center Honors; from live broadcasts of the Oscars and the Democratic National Convention to Barbra Streisand's *Timeless*, and President Obama's Inaugural Concert at the Lincoln Memorial. And more recently the opening of the Smithsonian's National Museum of African American History and Culture on the National Mall in Washington.

So how did I, the son of a country boy from a Texas town best known for "Remember the Alamo," end up creating some of America's greatest celebrations? I had no show business or political connections. I was the first in my family to graduate from college and the first to leave Texas. And I was the first to embrace parts of America's culture that my family would never have known or cared about. How did all this happen?

WHEN TELEVISION CAME TO TOWN
A SEED WAS PLANTED

I was nine years old when my father took me to a basketball arena in San Antonio for the very first live broadcast of this much anticipated new medium—Television. WOAI TV, Channel 4, on the very first day of live television in South Texas, had singers and dancers performing in the middle of the basketball court. The performers were out there on the court with the cameras, lights, boom mikes, back lines of amplifiers, drum set-ups, grand pianos, and stage crews. Surrounding the court were hundreds of television sets pointing up into the bleachers. Dad and I sat there in the stands and watched country singers, square dancers, and mariachi bands performing on the court, while also watching them live on the television sets rimming the basketball court.

I was riveted and could hardly contain my excitement, my curiosity, and my wish it would never end. Never mind that I was only nine, I felt like this was where I wanted to be forever.

In those early years, television brought history, culture, and adventure into my life. Dave Garroway's *Wide Wide World* (a live NBC series in the early 1950s) took me to places around our planet that I never dreamed of seeing. Thrilled, I would sit and watch the test pattern before the evening programs began. Even that was mind blowing.

It was an exciting time—being a young boy coming of age as television was coming of age. While other boys were building forts with chairs and tables and playing cowboys and Indians, I was building a fantasy TV studio in my garage—cameras made from cardboard boxes, with empty toilet paper spools for lenses, lights clamped to ladders, and curtains made out of old bedspreads. I thought of myself as a cameraman and director; the neighbors thought of me as that "strange Mischer kid."

During my early teens I played my steel guitar in several San Antonio bands—The Rhythm Ranch Hands, Boots Yates and the Texas Plowboys, George Chambers and the Country Gentleman. We often played on local television, and anytime I walked into a TV studio, even though I had come to play, I was more mesmerized by the workings of the television studio. My heart just raced.

I often daydreamed about making a living in television but couldn't see how that might become a possibility.

In high school, my father (and other family members) discouraged me. Dad was in the insurance business, and because I had an aptitude in math, he thought I'd make a great actuary. One day we had a serious talk about it, and I simply said, "Dad, I just don't see my life's work being spent calculating the probability of death for smokers, pilots, or mountain climbers for an insurance company."

Despite television's allure, I went on to college and received a master's degree from the University of Texas in Austin in 1963 and had a grant from the Hogg Foundation in Houston to continue toward a PhD in Sociology and Political Science. I assumed I'd become a college professor, but on Friday, November 22nd, 1963, a tragedy in Dallas would change my life forever.

TELEVISION BRINGS US TOGETHER
AFTER PRESIDENT KENNEDY'S ASSASSINATION

On Friday, November 22nd, 1963, a bunch of my college buddies and I headed to Bergstrom Air Force Base outside of Austin to join throngs of people in welcoming President Kennedy and First Lady Jacqueline Kennedy to the Texas Capital after their motorcade in Dallas. Once they arrived, President Kennedy was to speak at the University of Texas before he and Jackie headed west to spend the weekend with Vice President Lyndon Johnson and his wife Lady Bird at their ranch in the Texas Hill Country. Endless rows of chairs were already filling up and overflowing on the plaza in front of the campus tower as the university eagerly waited to greet the handsome, vibrant, articulate young president of the United States.

It wasn't until my buddies and I arrived at the base that we heard the news—President Kennedy had been shot in Dallas. We raced to a nearby TV screen and joined the crowd that was gathered there in stunned silence, and together we all watched Walter Cronkite, trying hard to control his emotions, remove his glasses and announce in a broken voice, "From Dallas, Texas, the flash apparently official: President Kennedy died at 1:00 PM Central Standard Time—2:00 Eastern Standard Time—some thirty-eight minutes ago."

Oh, my God! So many feelings all at once, it was impossible to process them. Shock. Grief. Disbelief. And for me, anger. "God damn this state. Why did this have to happen in Texas? Of course, if it was going to happen anywhere, it would happen here."

A day later, an emotionally disturbed ex-Marine named Lee Harvey Oswald, who had once defected to Russia, was arrested in a Dallas movie theater, and ultimately charged with the assassination of the president. Oswald was taken to the Dallas Police Station, which was like the Wild West—people just hung around the DPD, often carrying guns, and strange things happened there. Jack Ruby, a night club owner, not a cop, had complete run of the place. On the day Oswald was brought in for questioning, Jack Ruby was there to watch. As Oswald was being escorted in, Ruby casually walked over, pulled a gun out of his pocket, and shot Oswald dead at point blank range. Oswald's murder was caught on the live news feeds and seen around the world! The DPD quickly became a joke. "What would happen if an elephant walked into the Dallas Police Department?" The answer—"Nothing."

Television broadcasts a lot of mediocre and extraneous stuff. But sometimes, in moments of tragedy, it can become a source of information and shared emotion. A united country watched Vice President Lyndon Johnson assuming office as our new president on Air Force One, Jackie Kennedy still in her blood-stained, pink Chanel suit and in utter shock, standing by his side, a little more than two hours after her husband was killed.

The events of that weekend? Staggering and gut-wrenching and deeply disturbing. Then, two days later we all cried as John Kennedy Jr., just three days from his third birthday, saluted his father's casket as it rolled past the White House on Pennsylvania Avenue on its way to Arlington National Cemetery.

Television had been around for fourteen years or so, but that weekend I believe it came of age. We saw and lived its power. We became a nation in mourning and we shared our collective grief while watching minute-by-minute coverage on live TV. It brought us together in our darkest hour.

Almost immediately after President Kennedy's assassination, TV news crews began descending on Austin, a little more than a half hour away from our new president's ranch. It was immediately apparent as we watched Lyndon Johnson being sworn in, that compared to the polished, highly educated glamor of the Kennedys, LBJ came across as something of a country bumpkin. But who was this Lyndon Johnson guy? How did people feel about him? How did he come to power? What was his lifestyle? America wanted to know, and these news crews were charged with finding out.

They needed help and they needed it now. As a political science major at the University of Texas, I was hired as a guide and gofer to drive producers and directors around Austin and to LBJ's nearby ranch. I was blown away by these guys. They were smart, decisive, and they moved fast. Within an hour of arriving in Austin, they were already feeding stories to the world about America's new president.

Those few days were an emotional rollercoaster for me but staying busy helped me deal with my grief about losing a young, erudite president that I loved. They also lit a fire in me. I'd experienced the excitement of live television before, in studios, and stadiums, and along parade routes. But there was something about watching it being made that made my heart beat faster. I'd wondered in passing from time to time if I could make a living in television but I'd just been afraid to try. It was too risky. The assassination of John Kennedy changed all of that. For better or for worse, I put my PhD on hold, and I decided to give television—and its endless possibilities—a shot. And so, my journey began.

My life over the next six decades would weave through wild successes and heartbreaking failures—there was agony and ecstasy. But never once did I regret the decision. I loved all of it. The ups and downs. The stress and high risks. Rolling the dice every time you counted down to a high-profile live broadcast such as the Olympic Opening Ceremonies, Super Bowl halftime shows, or the Oscars. I considered myself blessed to be earning a living doing something I was so crazy about.

What follows are selected stories, as I have remembered them over my sixty-year career—stories of extraordinary moments in television as seen through my eyes. Yes, I was in the catbird's seat (a phrase coined by James Thurber in a 1942 short story)—a position of oversight and in many ways one that allowed me to act as an eyewitness to history. These are my stories.

MICHAEL JACKSON
MOONWALKING INTO HISTORY

As a kid who grew up on the segregated soil of Texas in the 1940s and '50s, I never thought when I left home that one day, I'd be directing one of the most famous events in Black music history, with the songs and performers that swept up all of young America. You never know where the road will take you, which is what made my life in television the great adventure it was.

In the winter of 1959, Berry Gordy, a young Black man from Detroit, Michigan who was about to turn thirty, started a record company called Motown. It was named after the Motor City of his birth, and it would forever change American music. It's impressive that so many of our greatest performers, singers, and songwriters began their careers at Motown, under the not-always-benign guidance of Mr. Gordy. The Jackson 5, Marvin Gaye, Diana Ross and the Supremes, Stevie Wonder, the Temptations, the Four Tops, Gladys Knight and the Pips, Smokey Robinson and the Miracles, and the husband-and-wife song-writing team of Nick Ashford and Valerie Simpson—those are only some of the jewels in the crown of Motown.

Berry Gordy had created one of the most influential sounds of the twentieth Century, and when Gordy's Motown label was turning twenty-five it was time to acknowledge and celebrate this extraordinary achievement. It was to be called, not surprisingly, *Motown 25: Yesterday, Today, Forever*. *M25* was to be built around its musical significance— the soundtrack of twenty-five years in the life of our unique and troubled land, music that was—and is—a fount of joy as well as a shout for freedom and justice. This explosion of great American music involved me in 1983 as it approached its twenty-fifth Anniversary.

Berry Gordy was a trailblazer, a short man with a big infectious smile. He's someone who always challenged conventional thinking. For example, when making records Berry often selected takes that were not musically perfect. Many times, I heard him say—"A clinker in the horn section? Doesn't bother me if I think the overall feeling is right." The first time I met with Berry to discuss co-producing and directing *Motown 25*, was after I was contacted by Suzanne de Passe, the President of Motown Productions. (Suzanne is also credited with discovering the Jackson 5 and thus Michael Jackson). The meeting was in his office on the twenty-second floor in a building next to the Hollywood Palladium on Sunset Boulevard in Los Angeles. Motown occupied the entire top two floors. His office was dark mahogany and elegantly decorated with memorabilia, Gold Records, Grammy Awards and art. (I heard that Berry had a secret room behind his desk. I think he could press a button and a wall would open up for access to this space.) But most of my meetings were at Berry's lavish estate on top of a hill in Bel Air, an exclusive community in West Los Angeles. He owned the whole hill. It was like a ranch in the middle of Los Angeles—a stunning environment, complete with his private zoo where he kept, among other animals, giraffes, exotic birds, and even a tiger.

When Berry Gordy and Suzanne de Passe made their decision and took a white guy from Texas under their wing for Motown's 25th, I was honored beyond belief. I grew up in the 1940s and '50s in a totally segregated Texas city—San Antonio—so how the hell did I get so lucky? The rise of Motown was one of the major cultural currents of the twentieth Century and now I got the chance to help tell the story.

I felt blessed, and many of the relationships I made on *Motown 25* have lasted for a lifetime.

We taped the extravaganza at the Pasadena Civic Auditorium before a live audience—how could it be done any other way? It aired on NBC on May 16, 1983. But by1983, many of the Motown artists— Michael Jackson and his brothers (the Jackson 5), Stevie Wonder, Lionel Richie, Diana Ross, Marvin Gaye, and Smokey Robinson— had left the Motown label. They all agreed to come back and celebrate twenty-five years of Motown music, but the catch was they wanted to sing their current music as well as their older Motown hits. Marvin Gaye wanted to sing "Sexual Healing" which had been released by Columbia Records in 1982, but we felt that was wrong—this was about Motown, pure and simple. Then Suzanne de Passe worked her magic. She said no to Marvin Gaye and somehow got all the other artists to agree to come back and just sing one of their Motown songs.

It was a glorious night of reunions. Smokey Robinson reunited with the Miracles to sing "My Momma Done Told Me" and "Shop Around," the Four Tops and the Temptations battled with "Papa Was a Rollin' Stone" and "Sugar Pie, Honey Bunch," and Diana Ross reunited with the Supremes for their hit, "Stop! In the Name of Love."

But there was one artist we really needed to make this show work— Michael Jackson, and Michael came with preconditions! We asked him to come back with his brothers, re-uniting the Jackson Five; singing Motown hits like, "I'll be There," "Never Can Say Goodbye," and "I Want You Back." To our relief, he said okay.

"But," Michael added emphatically, "you've got to let me sing one new song." Well, that would mean everyone else would want to do a new song, so how could we do that? We came very, very close to saying no to Michael Jackson. Suzanne and I joked, "Who's going to take the call from Marvin Gaye on Monday when he says, 'you told me I

couldn't do 'Sexual Healing,' but you let Michael sing his new song!'"
Nonetheless, Suzanne wanted to check out Michael's moves during his
new song on the stage. After we finished rehearsing the night before
the show, we emptied the theater at midnight, leaving only Suzanne,
me, Smokey Robinson, Linda Ronstadt, and a couple of others in the
theater. We watched as Michael stepped on the stage and performed
"Billie Jean." We were speechless. It was spellbinding. Suzanne and I
said almost at the same time, "I'll take the call from Marvin Gaye on
Monday." So Suzanne and Berry agreed, and Michael Jackson's "Billie
Jean" was slotted into the show.

The *Motown 25* event was rough for me in the truck. I felt as if I
never got a handle on it. Richard Pryor, our host, just disappeared as
we began taping the show—no—where to be found. Stevie Wonder's
musicians and vocalists were set on stage because he was opening the
show. But thirty minutes before we started, Reggie, Stevie's manager,
called me in the truck and said, "Hey man. We're not going to make it
there tonight, but I promise we'll be there first thing tomorrow morning." I said, "But Reggie, the show is tonight. Stevie's band is already
set up on the stage, and you're on in thirty-five minutes. Where the hell
are you guys? There is no tomorrow!" Reggie replied, "Okay. Okay,
we will try to get there before midnight." So, the first thing we did in
front of our audience—very hyped up and anticipating the show was
to stop and strike Stevie's massive set-up. And that was just the beginning. We had lots of starts and stops. I called them "hiccups." I hated
"hiccups" because they brought the momentum in the room to a complete stop. I took pride in keeping my shows moving like a theatrical
event—no stops and starts. During one "hiccup" midway through the
show, two cops from the Pasadena Police Department came into the
truck and asked, "Are you Don Mischer?"

"Yes?"

"We want you to know that we just arrested Diana Ross's band for cocaine possession, and they are at the station house on Garfield Avenue." Jesus. What next?

I always tend to overreact to difficult positions I find myself in and, of course, this was no exception. Despite some incredibly amazing moments, I left the Pasadena Civic Auditorium that night in a funk. I felt obligated to go to the after party across the street where cast and crew were happy and celebrating, but I just couldn't make myself do it. I walked back to my hotel room and collapsed.

As we began editing, it quickly became clear that I was dead wrong. *Motown 25: Yesterday, Today, and Forever* became a game changer. It would, in fact, become one of the best shows in my whole career.

But NBC was scared about airing *Motown 25*. When we delivered the first cut, NBC executives gave Suzanne and I notes, saying it was a good show but, "way too Black." They thought viewer demographics would skew Black and not really appeal to the diverse (i.e., white) audiences. They asked us if we could include white artists—Elton John, Mick Jagger, Paul McCartney—talking about how they had been influenced by Motown artists. Suzanne de Passe and I were certain that was not necessary, and we said, no! When *Motown 25* aired it got exceptionally high ratings and the best demographics of any show ever aired on NBC.

Stunning to say the least, and the reviews were raves across the boards. It received a Peabody Award, nine Emmy nominations, and won the Emmy for Best Variety show of the year. Can't do much better than that!

On show night I was directing in the truck, and I'll never forget the moment after the Jackson 5—Michael's brothers—left the stage. Michael stood alone saying, "That was the old; now here's some of the new." Suddenly he struck a pose—the cocked fedora, the black sequined jacket, and the white glove that all these years later can now be seen under glass at the Smithsonian Institution.

"Billie Jean" began, instantly recognizable after seven weeks on the Billboard charts. But Michael had something else in mind, something that he had been practicing, surprisingly, at the home of Sammy Davis, Jr. When he came to the bridge of "Billie Jean," he suddenly appeared to defy some physical law, moving backwards, as if he were dancing on a different and weightless planet. It was "the moonwalk." Mikhail Baryshnikov, the extraordinary dancer who defected from Russia and became one of the greatest dancers of the twentieth century, would later say that Michael's performance that evening—and the moonwalk in particular—was one of the greatest pieces of dance he had ever seen.

Michael had kept the dance move a great secret. Of course, after that night, he would never be allowed to retire the move. It would be his moon shadow, following him around the world. Curiously, "Billie Jean" was the only song Suzanne de Passe and Berry Gordy allowed to be sung that wasn't a Motown recording. Partly because Michael had just released "Thriller," produced by Quincy Jones, and it was quickly becoming an international phenomenon, one of the best-selling records in history. Even Berry Gordy couldn't refuse Michael Jackson, not then.

After the taping, Michael said he wanted to edit "Billie Jean" sitting next to me in the editing room. He clearly wanted control. I called him in a few days ahead to say we'd begin the editing of "Billie Jean" on April 12 at Complete Post on Sunset Boulevard, at 2:00 PM. At 11:00 AM that day, two lawyers made a surprise visit to our edit bay and quietly took a seat in the back. Yes, they were

's attorneys. Michael himself arrived a little before 2:00 PM and together we went through "Billie Jean," shot by shot—discussing every option. After three hours, Michael was happy, and so was I. As we walked out of the edit bay he stopped me in the hallway, where we were alone. He looked me in the eye and said, "You're not going to change anything after I'm gone, are you?" I assured him I wouldn't.

Michael Jackson and I developed a mutual trust and worked on numerous shows together including his 1993 Super Bowl halftime at the Rose Bowl in Pasadena, which Michael demanded I direct despite NBC Sport's objection. NBC had never allowed anyone other than the sports director of the game shoot the halftime show. So, for me to direct it would break decades of precedent. But Michael had been in show business his entire life. He knew what he wanted and how to get it. "Either Don sits in the director's chair, or I'm not doing it," Michael demanded. Michael held firm, and Dick Ebersol, President of NBC Sports, finally had to agree. Michael and I continued with many other productions until his untimely death at age fifty on June 25th, 2009. That was a sad day for me. Michael carried the weight of being the breadwinner for the Jackson Family ever since he was six years old. The pressure he was under was relentless, and it eventually got to him.

Michael's performance of "Billie Jean" became iconic. *Rolling Stone* recently wrote that it still ranks as one of the best moments in pop history. *Entertainment Weekly* called it, "a watershed moment in our cultural history." Diana Ross said of that night, "we had no idea how historic that evening would prove to be."

Marvin Gaye had left Motown in 1982, then signed with Columbia Records for whom he'd recorded "Sexual Healing" in 1983. But all was forgiven, at least that evening, when Marvin watched Michael Jackson's electrifying performance of "Billie Jean." Marvin later appeared on-stage seated at the piano and gave the audience something of a history lesson in Black music, after which, stepping away from the piano he sang his extraordinary, pleading anthem, "What's Going On." I remember Marvin conveying so much grace and pain, I had the camera just stay tight on his expressive face—it was powerful! It would be his last national appearance on television before he was shot and killed by his own father the following year.

I'll never know if it was working with the Motown artists that won me my stripes with the Black music community, but a few years later, I was working with another iconic African American musical genius, on the open-air stage of the Super Bowl halftime.

PRINCE IN THE RAIN
WORKING WITH A GENIUS

I t had started raining by the time I got back to the hotel at 1:00AM on Sunday morning, February 4th, 2007. It was Super Bowl Sunday. We were in Miami working with Prince on the halftime show at Super Bowl XLI (2006). I needed to sleep, but I couldn't. Light rain was predicted for the game, and I was scared. Prince's stage was shaped like his logo; it took 620 volunteers to roll out seventeen giant pieces of the stage onto the field and fit them together like a giant jigsaw puzzle. The surface of the stage was shiny mylar that was slippery to begin with, and when it got wet, it could be dangerous. Dolphin Stadium in Miami Gardens had no roof. Both the game and the halftime show were fully exposed to the elements.

My head was rattling with problems that rain could cause. For one thing, Prince was to play four live electric guitars. Would they short out? Would they stay in tune when sopping wet? The Twinz, Prince's spectacular identical twin dancers, would be wearing stiletto heels that were eight inches high. What would happen if one of them fell and got injured? Would we stop and bring out a stretcher? Or would we barrel through with just one of the Twinz? How odd would that be?

My line of work is high risk. People who do what I do are always taking chances. Often on the night before a show, I think to myself, "You've been really lucky, man. You've had people jumping out of helicopters, flying on thin wires high above the Oscar audience at the Dolby Theater in Hollywood, and standing in very scary places—like on top of towering skinny buttes of red sandstone in Arizona's Monument Valley—and so far, no one has ever fallen or suffered serious injury. Moreover, no one ever died! But sometimes I feel like I've been dodging bullets my whole career. What? Me worry? Well ... it's just part of the job."

When I first met Prince at his house on Sierra Alta Way in Beverly Hills, I parked in his driveway, and he personally greeted me at the door. I was expecting his house to feel "rock and roll," but what I saw was elegance and sophistication. Art and fresh flowers were everywhere. His logo, which was a "love symbol" mash-up of the gender symbols for a man and a woman, was embedded in his entryway with tiny gold and purple tiles. It was amazing. And just off the entryway there was a huge, fully equipped elevated sound stage with instruments set and ready to go on a moment's notice, and state of the art recording, editing, and mixing gear. He kept two tech ops (operators) 24/7 at his house. If Prince had a creative idea in the middle of the night, it was, "Everybody up!"

He walked me to his dining room, and we sat down. He was soft spoken and a gentleman. He looked me in the eye and said, "We'll be working together for months, and I want you to know that there is absolutely no alcohol or profanity in my presence." A little surprised by his request, I respectfully nodded.

For Super Bowl XLI, his artistic objectives were different from any previous halftime artists, who always chose to sing only their own songs. Prince clearly wanted a great show more than just promoting his own songs. So, he included songs from Bob Dylan, Foo Fighters, Queen, and John Fogerty, creating a unique, unpredictable show for a massive worldwide audience. When I pitched the Florida A&M Marching Band joining him on the field and suggested creating his silhouette against a billowing silk fabric, he liked those ideas, and we did them. We spent a lot of time thinking about pyrotechnics or "pyro" and decided to use it occasionally for accents, until the finale, when we would full out blow the stadium apart.

We all moved to Miami a week before the game and rehearsed on the actual stage—assembled in a large tent next to the stadium—for five hours a day. We had only one rehearsal on the actual Dolphin Stadium turf, and that was Thursday night three days before the game. It didn't go well. Prince was not happy. He couldn't hear his voice fold back to him on the stage speakers. He had trouble singing in the right key and staying in tempo.

We met in his trailer, and I asked, "Why didn't you just stop the rehearsal?"

He said, "I didn't know I could do that."

I was shocked and I felt I had dropped the ball. I should have discussed rehearsal objectives before we went out on the field. I said, "If you are bothered by something when we are rehearsing, we need to stop and fix it. That's what rehearsals are for." I continued, "You have to feel comfortable and confident when you're performing for millions of people around the world." I brought in our sound engineers. It was not a big deal and took no time to fix the fold back issue. Then we went back out on the field and spritzed water on the stage to see how slippery it got when wet. As expected, it was dangerously slippery. We all went home that night, concerned about safety.

Then, it was game day: Indianapolis Colts versus Chicago Bears. It was raining lightly, but the first half of the game went smoothly. At halftime, it was Colts 16 and Bears 14 as the players left the field. When the head referee signaled us that we now had control of the field, Gary Natoli, our lead stage manager, jumped into action. He had only six minutes and forty seconds to roll out and assemble the seventeen huge pieces of Prince's stage—complete with his band, lighting, wind machines, special effects, a couple of miles of audio cable, and a tiny dressing room for Prince under the stage, then bring 3,000 Prince fans onto the field, and finally, line up the Florida A&M Marching Band in the stadium tunnels. Our 620 volunteers had been rehearsing the stage roll out onto the field, assembly, sound and light checks, tear down, and roll off over and over at a nearby high school football field for a month. I'm convinced they were so familiar with the drill that they could have done it in a whiteout blizzard. So, as we were about to go on air, we were all set, and all seemed to be okay....

Then, about thirty seconds before air, the heavens just opened, and a torrential rainstorm hit. Prince was now preset under the stage. I called him on my walkie, "Just want to give you a heads-up...it's really coming down now."

Prince said to me, "Can you make it rain harder?" That amazed me. He clearly saw the downpour as a personal challenge. It wasn't going to stop him.

I said, "Okay...go for it!"

Gregg Gelfand, my associate director, started counting down, "10...9...8..." to air. I tried not to panic but I felt like the captain of an ocean liner just before he hits the iceberg.

We kicked off with a few seconds of Queen's "We Will Rock You." Then an explosion. Prince rose dramatically from center stage on an elevator lift called a "toaster" with "Let's Go Crazy." By the time we got ninety seconds into the show, by some miracle, the guitars were still working, the Twinz were still dancing, and rain was hitting the hot lights on and around the stage, creating an ethereal mist of smoke and steam drifting across the stage and into the crowd. Water droplets hitting the camera lenses created a surreal look of hexagonal twinkling stars. It was haunting. A look we could never have dreamed of—and all because of the heavy rain. Prince grabbed his doo-rag and threw it into the audience, allowing the water droplets to run down his face. Thrilled at what I was seeing, I yelled to several cameras, "Get me real tight close-ups!"

Suddenly, I realized that our biggest fear—the rain—had become a blessing—a magical act of nature that inspired Prince to deliver one of his best performances ever. If I ever needed proof that live television is unpredictable, that sometimes things do go wrong, this was the time. Instead, it was spectacular. And it kept getting better as Prince powered his way through John Fogerty's "Proud Mary." And then dramatically changed pace with Bob Dylan's "All Along the Watchtower." During "The Best of You" (Foo Fighters) we used six old prop airplane engines mounted flat into the stage to blow upward a thirty-five-foot high silk fabric. It was soaking wet and much heavier than we wanted, but thankfully it rose. On it we projected a huge live silhouette of Prince playing his guitar behind it. Dave Grohl, the lead singer and guitarist for Foo Fighters later said, "Having been a massive fan of Prince my whole life, I was flattered beyond words. What an honor to be covered by one of your heroes."

I was later told that a lighting cable had been severed when the stage was being rolled out onto the field. The severed cable had controlled half of the stage lights. Tony Ward, head gaffer of our lighting crew, worked feverishly and unsuccessfully to fix it, and about a minute before air, he just gave up and stripped the insulation off of three copper wires, inserted them into a female plug, and held them together while standing next to the stage for twelve and a half minutes in the pouring rain. I'm thankful I didn't know it at the time—there was enough stress as it was. But Tony Ward saved the show.

By the time we got to the finale, 85,000 people—soaking wet and bathed in purple light—were on their feet singing, "Purple Rain" with Prince. It was magical. In the truck, Bruce Rodgers, who had designed and built the set, and fellow producer Glenn Weiss were standing behind me—mesmerized. How lucky could we get? On the last note of "Purple Rain," I used a chopper high above Dolphin Stadium to shoot the extraordinary pyro finale which wrapped around the entire stadium.

Wow! The response was instant. Thirty seconds after going off the air, calls flooded into the truck from all around the country and the world—even from Australia and China, where it was 7:00 AM Monday morning. Prince had scored big time.

After coming down from the high, I took my wife, Suzan, my son, Charlie, and my daughter, Lilly, to visit Prince backstage. He and I were both relieved. We chatted for a bit and when we said goodbye, Prince glanced at me and then said to Suzan, "You've got a good one here." As strange as it may sound, that made me feel validated by a genius artist I was both honored and proud to be working with. Prince put his heart and soul into that show. The *New York Times* said, "his performance last night at Super Bowl XLI will surely go down as one of the most thrilling halftime shows ever."

And it has—to this day.

WHEN SUPER BOWL HALFTIMES BECAME THE ARTIST'S SHOWCASE

In 1992, Super Bowl XXVI (26) was played in the Hubert H. Humphrey Metrodome in Minneapolis, Minnesota on January 26th, 1992—the Washington Redskins played the Buffalo Bills. The telecast of the game on CBS was seen by an estimated 79.6 million viewers. But more importantly, this was the first time that a major television network successfully counter-programmed a Super Bowl halftime show. CBS called their halftime show "Winter Magic," with hundreds of dancers running around as snowflakes, joined by Brian Boitano and Dorothy Hamill (Olympic gold medal ice skaters). But because there was no place to ice skate on the football field, Brian and Dorothy ended up just singing while the University of Minnesota Marching Band paraded around them. It was a strange concept to say the least. Meanwhile Fox heavily promoted a special live football-themed episode of its popular Black sketch comedy show In Living Color. They encouraged viewers to flip over to Fox for a fun halftime, and then flip back to the game on CBS in at the beginning of the third quarter. That's exactly what fans did.

As the players ran off the field at halftime, millions of fans—a major portion of the CBS television audience—did, in fact, switch to Fox. The *In Living Color* Fox special pulled twenty to twenty-five million viewers away from the Super Bowl. The Nielsen ratings service estimated that CBS lost ten ratings points during halftime as viewers switched over to Fox. More importantly, the viewers never came back for the second half of the football game because by the end of the second quarter, the Redskins had jumped out to a 17-0 lead from which the Bills never recovered.

This was a major wake up call for the NFL. The Super Bowl halftime show could no longer be a filler in the middle of America's premier football game. The National Football League and the host network had to come up with Super Bowl halftime shows featuring the absolute top names in entertainment—stars that would unequivocally hold their audience with no chance viewers would have any desire to change channels or sample something else. This was the first step in making Super Bowl halftime shows one of the most desirable gigs for artists anywhere in the world.

One year later in 1993, the Super Bowl was played in Pasadena at the Rose Bowl. Radio City Productions was hired to deliver a top name. And they did—Michael Jackson! Couldn't do much better than that. But Michael insisted that Don Mischer Productions produce the show with me sitting in the director's chair. This raised some problems. First, it diluted Radio City's control, and secondly, NBC Sports said they would never let a non-sports director sit in their trucks directing a Super Bowl halftime show. A tug of war ensued until Michael Jackson flat out demanded, "If Don is not sitting in the director's chair, I'm not doing it." Dick Ebersol, President of NBC Sports, was a friend of mine, and he took pains to explained to me why he couldn't let me direct it. The halftime show, he told me, "Must be directed by a sports director because it's part of a major sporting event, and it's been that way since the beginning."

So, I then tried to talk to Michael to ease his uncertainty saying, "Michael, I can sit right next to the NBC sports director John Gonzales. He's a good guy. We can work out the staging and shooting of the halftime show and you will be fine with it." But Michael flatly refused to perform if I wasn't sitting in the director's chair—by myself. Michael's refusal to consider any other alternatives continued for weeks. Nobody ever said no to Michael Jackson. When he wanted something, he got it. The stand-off dragged on for several more weeks. Michael Jackson stood firm and unyielding. Period! Finally, not wanting to lose such a premiere talent for their halftime show, NBC finally capitulated, agreeing that I and my associate director, Allan Kartun, could jump into the football truck during the commercial break at the halftime, direct the show, then quickly get out of the football truck before the third quarter began. That's what happened. And it worked beautifully. The Jackson halftime show was so successful that NBC sports decided for all future Super Bowl halftime shows to bring in entertainment producers/directors. And that's the way it remains now—thirty years later.

Today, artists are keenly aware of what a halftime show at the Super Bowl can do for their brand. They are paid nothing, just expenses. However, they get twenty-five to thirty-five million dollars in exposure (when compared to what commercials cost during the halftime show), and they always get a giant spike in record sales. Beyoncé's record sales jumped 230 percent in the week after her Super Bowl XLVII (47) halftime. Maroon 5 saw a 485 percent jump after their Super Bowl LIII (53) in 2019. And all Super Bowl performers gain millions of new followers on social media. Bradford Cobb, Katy Perry's manager, said of her halftime show in 2015, "It took her from being just a pop star right into the stratosphere."

But as the director, I had to make sure the artists accepted the conditions necessary to perform in the Super Bowl halftime show. First, they would not have unilateral control the way they do when touring with their own shows. Secondly, the Super Bowl halftime show is just one cog in a giant wheel called Super Bowl Sunday, and the artists must accept that. I recall the first meeting we had with Michael Jackson, the NFL, and NBC in planning the halftime for Pasadena's upcoming Super Bowl XXVII (27) in 1993. Michael, always soft-spoken, walked into the room, graciously shook everyone's hand, sat down at the head of the table, and began by saying, "I want to move the start time of the game three hours later so my halftime show will be at night instead of in full sunlight."

There was silence in the room. I then jumped in and tried to explain to Michael how that would mean that viewers in the Eastern and Central time zones (eighty percent of the country) would have to stay up until after midnight to see the end of the game—no way, of course, that that was going to happen. Then there was a strict time limit—twelve minutes and thirty seconds. Also, the artist had to accept the "family" nature of the Super Bowl audiences...twenty percent of the viewers would be kids twelve years of age or younger.

By 1993, Michael had a stunning collection of big-time hits—"Beat It," "Thriller," "Wanna Be Startin' Something," and "Billie Jean." For every single one of his hits, his choreography was breathtaking, innovative, and mesmerizing. One of his favorite moves was grabbing his crotch while thrusting his hips forward. It's just what he did, and it was innocuous. But when he did the Super Bowl halftime in 1993, I worried about it. We had several private conversations about his grabbing his crotch. I told him he would get criticized for it because the Super Bowl halftimes were such "family-centric" events. He explained that when he performed his pop hits, "he just had to do it the way he always had," including occasionally grabbing his crotch. But if he sang something else—a ballad or a "feel good" song like "Heal the World," he would not be grabbing his crotch.

This being the first Super Bowl halftime show with a major artist, we were breaking new ground when it came to staging it. Joe Zenas (working with scenic designer Bob Keene) was given the task of designing and constructing this stage. Joe designed a masterful creation while having to serve many masters in doing so. Joe's stage weighed twelve tons, came out in twenty-six pieces, and had Michael's band and sound gear on board, including embedded lighting, pyro, special effects, and wind machines not to mention a small dressing room for MJ. We had only 5:30 seconds to roll it out onto the field, link the pieces together, and connect dozens of electric cables and sound check it. Most importantly, we had to promise the NFL that absolutely no damage would be done to the grass itself. Joe Zenas did a masterful job in designing the stage, including constructing it on low pressure balloon tires that would protect the field for the second half of the game. Joe and his team of volunteers spent four weeks at a nearby high school football field rolling it out, assembling it, taking it apart, and rolling it off the field—over and over again. We had only one shot at this, and we didn't want to embarrass ourselves in a high-profile event seen by over a billion people.

Michael Jackson and I had agreed that at the top of the halftime show, he would make a surprise entrance. As we hit zero on the countdown, a Michael Jackson double would pop up on top of the North Jumbotron at the Rose Bowl. Seconds later, a second Michael double would pop up on top of the South Jumbotron. Then at midfield, on a single pyro blast, the real Michael would pop out of the stage on a "toaster"—a spring triggered lift under the stage that catapulted him high above the stage surface. He would land back on the stage and froze with his hands at his side. The crowd would go nuts! Michael wanted to "sense" the crowd reaction before he started singing. He and I agreed that I would not cue his musicians until he gave me the sign—he would slowly reach up and touch his sunglasses, and then I would cue Jennifer Batten, his lead guitarist, to hit her opening licks. Okay. Fine. That should work, I thought.

So, on game day we count down to going on the air. 10...9...8...7. The doubles popped up on top of the Jumbotrons, then a big explosion and Michael (on the toaster) popped up at center stage and froze. The crowd was hysterical, and he stood there—perfectly still—with 90,000 people in the Rose Bowl anticipating his much talked about performance. We waited—ten, eleven, twelve seconds. After twenty seconds, I started getting nervous. There was a lot of screaming and yelling from the 3,500 MJ fans we put on the field surrounding the stage. We hit thirty seconds and Michael was still frozen. That is a long, long time. I started to yell at him through my intercom but I should have known he'd never hear me above all the fans. I yelled anyway, "Come on Michael, Go! Go! Go! Gimmie the cue, damn it!" Nothing! We waited. A minute had now passed, and I was losing it. "Come on, Michael! Do it for Christ's sake!" Finally, after one minute and thirty-five seconds (an eternity in live television), his hands slowly rose to touch his sunglasses, and I cued Jennifer to start her guitar licks, and we were off and running. The cheers that erupted in the truck were probably as loud as the cheers in the Rose Bowl. He did a medley of his pop hits (with some crotch grabbing) and then changed pace with "Heal the World," which triggered a card stunt of the children of the world, designed by school children in Los Angeles. Michael was stunning. He really nailed it.

At that time, Michael's show was the highest rated television event in history, with 1.3 billion viewers worldwide. The show was a big success. *USA Today*'s review called it dazzling but also mentioned that Michael grabbed his crotch eleven times. Oh well! For the next ten years, MTV took over the Super Bowl halftime shows.

But in the MTV-produced 2004 Super Bowl halftime show starring Janet Jackson and Justin Timberlake, which I was watching from home, something went terribly wrong. It created a perfect storm of moral outrage with what would become known as the "Wardrobe Malfunction" or "Nipplegate."

Janet Jackson and Justin Timberlake were singing "Rock Your Body," and when Justin sang the final lyric, "Gonna have you naked by the end of this song," he pulled off part of Janet's costume revealing her right breast with a tiny nipple shield on it. The shot was on the air for less than a second, and CBS cut to a wide shot immediately. But the damage was done. It triggered a furious debate about indecency in broadcasting. The nation was hysterical. MTV, which had produced the show, was immediately fired by the NFL and told they would never produce another halftime show. Never! In addition, CBS's parent company Viacom and all its co-owned subsidiaries, MTV, and Infinity Broadcasting, enforced a blacklist of Janet Jackson's singles and music videos on many radio formats and music channels worldwide. The Federal Communications Commission (FCC) fined CBS $550,000 for an indecency violation because of the incident.

The following year, 2005, the NFL came back to us asking DMP to help them clean up the Super Bowl halftime shows. They realized they had given too much autonomy to MTV. But after the "wardrobe malfunction," the NFL took a much more active role in Super Bowl halftimes. Charles Coplin and Lawrence Randall were NFL's execs overseeing Super Bowl halftimes. The NFL was not about to let another wardrobe malfunction happen on their watch. We continued producing the Super Bowl halftimes, some with White Cherry Entertainment's Ricky Kirshner and Glenn Weiss, but I was in the director's seat for each of them—Paul McCartney, the Rolling Stones, Prince, Tom Petty, and Bruce Springsteen.

Before I began my run of halftime shows, I had been tested on the field of another worldwide arena—the Olympics Opening and Closing Ceremonies.

MUHAMMAD ALI
WOUNDED IN BODY, SOARING IN SPIRIT

In my business, the Olympics Opening Ceremonies are the dream, the jewel in the crown of live television. In 1992, I had put together a proposal with a few trusted colleagues and submitted it to the Atlanta Olympic Committee, hoping we might be considered to produce the 1996 Centennial Olympic Games Opening Ceremonies. I knew dozens of much larger companies had submitted proposals, so getting it was an extreme long shot, and I went on with other jobs.

One morning, when I was directing an episode of *Murder, She Wrote* on the Universal lot, shooting a scene with Angela Lansbury and guest star, Mickey Rooney, I got a message saying, "There's a very important call coming in for you in five minutes." I finished the scene, told everyone to take a break and awaited this mysterious phone call. It was Billy Payne, head of the Atlanta Committee for the Olympic Games. He said, "Fifty-odd companies applied to produce the 1996 Olympic Ceremonies, but we chose you. Congratulations!"

I have to tell you, it was one of the most euphoric feelings ever. I think I ended up back on the set without my feet ever touching the ground. I just walked on air. I called my wife Suzan, a vice president at CBS, and told her to drive over right away, so I could tell her in person. This was too big to share over the phone. I joyfully called my colleagues David Goldberg, Kenny Ortega, Geoff Bennett, Sara

Lukinson, and Peter Minshall who had helped create our proposal. The Olympics were three years away, but we couldn't lose a minute.

That night the enormity of it hit me. Our four-hour Opening Ceremonies on July 19th, 1996 would be seen by 85,000 people in the stadium, and an estimated eighty percent of the entire world, reaching more than five billion people. It was the world's biggest stage. These would be the first summer games America had hosted since the 1984 games in Los Angeles—and only the fourth time in Olympic history for the Games to be hosted by an American city.

The Opening Ceremony carries the hopes and pride of the country. This is not where you want to screw up. If you do, you embarrass the host city, the country, and have a black mark against you for the rest of your career. It was a great honor to be chosen, but also a terrifying one. My way of handling those feelings is to immediately get to work. With a thousand things to think about, the one thing that woke me up every morning was the lighting of the Olympic Flame.

For me, that is the most climactic moment in the Opening Ceremonies, the emotional highpoint that everyone remembers most. The tradition of the flame dates to ancient Greece. In the modern games, the flame is lit by rays of the sun hitting a mirrored parabolic reflector in the ancient stadium in Olympia. Soon after the first rays of sunlight, a wick in the center of the parabolic mirror ignites in the intense reflected heat, giving birth to the Olympic flame. Over the next three months, the flame is relayed around the globe, touched by a thousand hands, and bringing the good wishes of the world.

When it reaches the stadium, the torch lights the cauldron that burns for the sixteen days of the games, symbolizing the Olympic spirit of competing in the name of sportsmanship and fellowship. It's the closest thing we have to a universal symbol of coming together in peace, and lighting it is the greatest honor of the Olympic ceremony. A moment the world is waiting for.

I was in the Los Angeles Coliseum in 1984 when Rafer Johnson took the torch from the granddaughter of Jesse Owens, the Black athlete who shattered Hitler's theory of a superior Aryan race in the 1936 Berlin Olympics while Hitler himself was watching. Now, forty-eight years later in Los Angeles, Jessie Owens' granddaughter Gina Hemphill ran up the Coliseum's long flight of stairs, passed the torch to Rafer Johnson who lit the cauldron. It was heart-beating excitement but also moving. It carried history with it.

I strongly feel that for a large spectacle show to be truly great, to make a lasting memory, it has to reach people's hearts and not just dazzle their eyes. I always try to give the audience that lump in the throat as well as thrilling them with the pageantry.

I talked over some ideas with my team, and then with Dick Ebersol, chairman of NBC sports and a longtime colleague. After tossing around several names, one stuck. Muhammad Ali. Yes, of course, it had to be Ali. He was one of the most beloved, admired, and recognized figures in the world. A 1960 Olympic gold medal winner and three-time heavyweight champion, he was revered as a man, a sportsman, a legend, and hero. We knew he was suffering from Parkinson's disease, but we also knew his giant unique spirit burned so brightly in our history.

In my mind I knew Ali had to be a complete surprise. He hadn't been seen much since the onset of his illness, so no one would ever expect him to be the man to do it. What a wonderful surprise that would be for the world! There were only five of us who knew, and we made a pact—if we can get Ali, we would not tell our spouses, our kids, not even NBC's highly respected commentators, Bob Costas and Dick Enberg—absolutely no one. Of course, if the press got ahold of it, all would be ruined.

So many questions were rattling round in my head—could we keep this a secret? Could Ali physically handle lifting the torch? We were literally playing with fire on this. If this beloved champion slipped, got disoriented, dropped the burning torch on the ground, or worse yet dropped it on himself, what would we do? He couldn't even bend over to pick up the torch if he dropped it.

Part of our job is always to anticipate everything that might go wrong, and for this particular moment, that list was very long, starting with how he'd light it. The cauldron had been designed for a young athlete to run up eight flights of stairs to light the flame on the very top. Certainly, Ali couldn't climb up to the top of the cauldron. So, we had two choices. We could either get a younger American athlete who could run up the cauldron steps or we could try to create an ingenious, never-tried-before solution. For me, it was not so much about HOW we lit the cauldron, but WHO lit it—that's the emotional payoff. To pull off the unexpected and near impossible is what stirs us on and makes us better.

What I didn't expect was that Billy Payne, the head of the Atlanta Olympic Committee would not like the idea. Billy saw Ali, or at least was afraid his constituents would, as a draft dodger who reflected poorly on Atlanta, on Georgia, and on the country. Billy asked, "Why not use Evander Holyfield, the heavyweight champion boxer from Atlanta?" Holyfield was a good choice, but no match for Muhammad Ali.

I called Billy several times, doing my best to persuade him, assuage his fears, and have him see Ali as we knew the world would. Dick Ebersol did as well. After a month, Billy finally agreed, but not without some trepidation. The Atlanta committee felt if it didn't work, they would get the blame.

I thanked Billy profusely and added, "But remember, Billy, this must remain a complete surprise. You can't tell anyone including your wife, your kids, nobody." We were thrilled. Now, all we had to do was get Ali to agree. I'd worked with Ali before and knew you had to go through Howard Bingham, his biographer, photographer, and right-hand person. Howard was a good guy, and it was best to meet with him in person, but if he walked into our offices at Atlanta's Olympic Stadium, people would connect the dots and know we were talking about Ali.

So, we arranged a secret meeting with Howard in a garbage collection room—a dingy, damp cement block room three levels down under the stadium. My co-producer, David Goldberg, and I brought in a folding card table, several chairs, and a single bulb desk light, and there we sat surrounded by bags of garbage. I wondered if this was a little like what meeting Deep Throat during Watergate had been like.

Howard liked the idea and thought Ali would too. As we began to work out some of the details, I was afraid someone in Ali's camp might leak this, so I turned to Howard and said, "This deal is conditional. If this leaks out to the press, even as late as the morning of the Opening Ceremonies, we have the right to have someone else light the cauldron." Bingham agreed.

I had learned the hard way that if you build up too much expectation in advance, when the moment comes, people find it a bit of a letdown. You need that thrill of a surprise to catch the audience off guard and to get those gasps of delight, astonishment, and emotion.

We needed to find ways to secretly rehearse with Ali at the stadium, where we had 24/7 security guards because of concerns about terrorism. On July 11th, eight days before the Opening Ceremonies, we told the security teams to go home early—at midnight. At 3:00 AM that morning, Muhammad Ali and Howard Bingham drove up in a simple sedan, a rental car we had supplied—no shiny limo—no entourage—in an absolutely blacked-out stadium. Using flashlights, the two of them walked very slowly to the base of the Olympic cauldron. Ali gave me a playful fake punch in the stomach, which he often did when greeting people. He couldn't speak anymore, and his hands were shaking, but that enormous gleam still burst from his eyes.

This man, whose career had been built around his strength and agility, who'd been as light footed as a gazelle, was willing—happy— to stand in front of the entire world, physically diminished but undiminished in spirit, undaunted in his love of life and belief in the meaning of the Olympics, of people coming together in peace and friendship. I was focused on rehearsing with him, and not tiring him out, but another part of me was simply overwhelmed and touched by his presence.

Ali would be handed the torch by Olympic gold medalist swimmer, Janet Evans, but we couldn't rehearse with her because she would be yet another person who would know about Ali. I stood in for Janet as we worked out how Ali would get the torch. Our solution for how he would light the cauldron ended up being a simple one. After raising the torch, he would touch it to a swab soaked in alcohol that would travel up a wire to ignite the cauldron. This concept was created and operated by Ed Kish, a highly experienced rigger out of Los Angeles.

After rehearsing, I could tell Ali was comfortable with the choreography, which relieved me to no end. Then Howard took a picture of the two of us that Ali later shakily signed. The look on my face was one of happiness and near disbelief. For the first time I felt like this was actually going to happen.

The night of the ceremonies, I was directing the world feed from an underground control room in Centennial Olympic Stadium, facing a wall of television screens. As the Atlanta Symphony reached the final triumphant chords of Beethoven's "Ode to Joy" from his 9th Symphony, Muhammad Ali appeared on the top of the stadium rim under the cauldron—there was no announcer introduction or musical fanfare. I hit him with a single spotlight, and he just stood there raising the torch above his head while his body trembled with Parkinson's Syndrome. Nothing could ever equal that sight of Ali simply by himself.

It worked! It was a complete surprise. A hush fell across the entire stadium, as people wondered, was that who they thought it was? For twelve seconds the audience was gasping in anticipation at what they were seeing. Is that Muhammad Ali holding the Olympic torch up high? Then I cut to a close-up of Ali. His face appeared across the stadium's jumbo screens and on worldwide television. A gigantic roar, as the crowd erupted. A surprised Bob Costas said, "Look who gets it now!"

Dick Enberg exclaimed, "The Greatest ... oh, my!" As the cameras zoomed around the audience, I could see people both cheering and crying in joy. It was an emotionally breathtaking, goosebump inducing moment. Costas continued, "Once the most dynamic figure in sports—a gregarious man now trapped inside that mask created by Parkinson's syndrome. So in one sense a poignant figure, but look at it—still a great, great presence, still exuding nobility and stature. And the response he evokes is part affection, part excitement, but especially respect." Bob Costas' eloquence in describing this emotional moment gave me goosebumps as I watched it unfold in my control room underneath the stadium.

To this day, Muhammad Ali holding the torch for the world to see as a symbol of all that is inspiring and good in us, remains one of the most indelible and stirring moments in Olympic Ceremony history—certainly, the most iconic moment of the Atlanta Games. Ali—his body trembling, his heart and soul and courage soaring—will be remembered and cherished for decades to come. Helping to create that moment is one of the proudest achievements of my life.

Seven days after Muhammad Ali's lighting the Olympic cauldron, we were completely focused on the Closing Ceremonies, which generally are under-rehearsed and much less polished than the Opening. On the night of July 26th, we worked with our production staff in our stadium office under Centennial Olympic Stadium until about 11:00 PM. It was Friday night, so many on our team wanted to go out to party a bit. The gathering place, especially late at night, was always Centennial Olympic Park in downtown Atlanta. That night, Jack Black and the Heart Attack were playing a rock concert which began just after midnight. I was "wiped" and left the stadium office around 11:30 PM and drove straight to our apartment in Buckhead, a suburb North of downtown Atlanta. There was no traffic, and I made it in record time. David Goldberg, as he often did, stayed behind and worked into the early morning in our office. When I walked into our apartment, Suzan was still up, but I was a little sorry that our kids, three-year-old Charlie and one-year-old Lilly, were already asleep. It was silly of me to think that they would be up at midnight, of course. Suzan and I had a glass of wine and talked a bit, but I fell into a deep sleep in less than twenty minutes.

The phone rang at 1:25 AM. It was David. "I've been watching TV on a little set in my office," he said. "I just saw something blow up at Centennial Olympic Park! People are running around screaming...it's chaotic down there!"

"Oh, God, no!" I said to David. Three pipe bombs with three-inch nails embedded had been placed in a backpack and set next to a sound tower near the concert stage. At 1:20 AM on July 27th, the bombs exploded, killing two people, and injuring 111. We were shocked, to say the least. And devastated.

My first concern was our staff and my two daughters—Jennifer and Heather—who were working on the show and often went to Centennial Olympic Park. In a matter of minutes, we found out they were okay. But suddenly, we were no longer worrying about the bands, dancers, and musical acts that we hoped would celebrate the achievements of Olympic athletes in the closing, or how to dramatically extinguish the Olympic Flame in the finale act of the Closing Ceremonies. Now the focus of our efforts changed to how we could deal with this terrorist attack. Should we have a moment of silence in the Closing Ceremonies? Would Billy Payne mention the terrorist act in his closing remarks? Or would Juan Antonio Samaranch, president of the International Olympic Committee, bring it up? And how would we handle this tragedy and honor the victims while not taking away from the joy and celebration of the athletes' achievements during the Games?

A decision was made a few days later by the IOC and the Atlanta Olympic Committee to let President Samaranch speak about the preservation of the Olympic spirit even in the face of terrorism, as it had done in 1972 in Munich when the Palestinian terrorist group Black September attacked Israeli athletes in Olympic Village—eleven Israelis were killed. By the time the attack ended, seventeen people had died, including a German policeman and most members of Black September.

We had been soaring through the first week of the games in Atlanta, but the bombing in Atlanta's Centennial Park put us all on edge and definitely dampened our spirits. For me, it felt like a blanket had been pulled out from underneath me, and that I was now swimming against the tide.

We had put three years into planning the Olympic Opening and Closing Ceremonies, but now I was losing my confidence. Every night as I put my head down on my pillow, I couldn't help thinking—what's next?

DEEP IN THE HEART OF TEXAS
THE EARLY YEARS

I had no idea when I left Texas and headed into the world of television, that I would one day be lucky enough to land in the director's chair for some of the most famous events of my time. I hadn't even dared to dream such things. My family did not have much access to the outside world. They just worked. Worked hard. Most of them never heard of Prince or Michael Jackson. They didn't listen to music and only occasionally read newspapers or magazines. And I know they were bothered by my own unexpected journey out of Texas in the early 1960's.

My father, Elmer Frederick Mischer, was born in 1916 and grew up picking cotton, slopping hogs, and shucking corn. The Mischers were poor German immigrant farmers who settled in Fayette County, Texas, between San Antonio and Houston—a rural German enclave complete with German newspapers, beer halls, festivals (Octoberfest), and where German was spoken in schools and churches. Dad had seven brothers and sisters. Dad's mother passed away when he was eight years old and his father when he was twelve, leaving the eight children to fend for themselves. The oldest child in the family was my Aunt Delta, who was fourteen years old. Now parentless, she and my Uncle Herbert, age thirteen, had to run the family farm themselves. So, they dropped out of school. The younger six kids, including my father, got to go to school. Somehow this family of eight children managed by themselves. They had an aunt who lived seven miles away in La Grange, Texas who would drive out in her Ford Model T every Sunday afternoon to see how they were doing.

I remember going to their homestead, where my aunts and uncles lived, when I was a little boy. They had a stone well that went down to thirty-five feet to find drinkable water. There was no hand pump, so you dropped a wooden bucket down into the well and hauled it up by hand. If you wanted to have hot water, you had to heat it on the wood burning stove in the kitchen. There was no electricity, no plumbing, no phone, and an outhouse out by their garden. They used kerosene lamps to light the house at night, and in freezing weather they warmed rocks on the wood stove and put them under their bedcovers to keep themselves warm. It was a rough life.

My dad never showed his emotions to anyone in the family.

I never recall him saying to me, "I love you." Feelings just weren't expressed. Growing up, he and his brothers and sisters just grit their teeth and never stopped working the farm. For them, life was all about survival. Being a farm boy, my dad was not very sophisticated. He had big ears and a strong big nose, which he passed on to my brother, sister, and me! We're actually proud of it now. He had an amazing work ethic, was honest, completely dependable and loved his family although he had difficulty expressing his feelings directly.

At age seventeen, my dad picked cotton the whole month of July. He ended up in the hospital in critical condition with a life-threatening infection in his right shoulder from dragging heavy muslin bags of cotton through the rows. In those days, there were no antibiotics, and he almost died. While spending three weeks in the hospital, he made a promise to himself. If he survived, he was going to run away from the farm and try to find a better life in San Antonio. That's exactly what he did—a testament to his determination and perseverance. When he left the farm, he got a job in San Antonio cleaning house for a family.

During the day he attended a Business School and did his household chores in the early morning and after school. He slept in the garage.

My mother, Lillian Alma Hoey, was gregarious, fun, and active. Born and raised in San Antonio, her family was Irish, and she was a cheerleader in high school. She was tall and a bit lanky, good-looking, with beautiful eyes, and she loved to dance.

In high school, I was very active. I was in student government, a member of the National Honor Society and played on the basketball team. When I was eleven years old, I took steel guitar lessons and by the time I was thirteen, I was playing a double-neck Fender steel guitar with local country bands in San Antonio—everything from Hank Williams, Patsy Cline, Bob Wills, and Johnny Cash to Polkas, Waltzes, and Texas Swing. My mom and my dad used to come a lot of dances because I was too young to drive. Back then, I also had the leads in some of the school plays and I made leather belts on which I carved the names of relatives for holiday gifts. But hard as I worked, I was never part of the cool group in school.

Life on our street was good. Great neighbors who truly enjoyed being with one another. Lots of barbecues, holiday parties, trick-or-treating, and playing football in the middle of the street after Thanksgiving dinner. Life felt comfortable.

My dad bought a used motorboat so we could water ski and aqua plane. We loved hunting and fishing together and traveled extensively in our 1951 pink and gray Buick to the National Parks throughout the American west.

When I was twelve years old my father bought me an 8mm Bell and Howell camera which gave me opportunities to create my own movies all around the house and especially when we traveled to National Parks. The camera had a single frame exposure button which allowed me to lock it down on a tripod and do single frame photography, putting together little animated sequences. I made oranges and apples square dance, and ornate salt and pepper shakers twirl around on top of our shiny dining room table with graceful choreographic moves to classical music. I'd climb up on our roof with my 8mm camera and tripod locked down, and time-lapse the little puffy clouds that were building- up in the sticky Texas afternoon heat into heavy thunderstorms. My dad gave me a vintage 1930s wire recorder from his office that he was about to throw away, which I used to record my soundtracks.

One of my favorite films was *Rocky Mountain Adventures* featuring our annual trips to Rocky National Park near Estes Park in Colorado in the front range of the Rocky Mountains. It captured breathtaking scenery, rushing streams teaming with fish, lush green forests, meadows of stunning wildflowers and bountiful wildlife—elk, bears, bighorn sheep, and moose. For a kid growing up in Texas where summer temperatures were generally above 100° F, going to Rocky Mountain National Park was like going to heaven. Our annual trips got me interested in mountain climbing, eventually climbing every mountain in the front range of the Rocky's including Long's Peak, the fourteenth highest mountain in Colorado, and years later the imposing Matterhorn in the Swiss Alps.

That 8mm camera, which I now have in my office in Hollywood in a glass mounted display, still runs as well as the day I received it more than seventy years ago.

My mom and dad became very proud of our family films I had made over a period of years. Dad would invite executives from his insurance company to come over and sit out in our backyard, eat barbecue, drink Lone Star beer, and after the sun went down, watch the movies on a roll up screen outside along with the soundtracks that I recorded on my wire recorder. I would feed the sound through a fender amplifier that I used in playing my steel guitar. My father never said to me point blank, "Son, I'm really proud of what you're doing and what you've done," but he didn't have to. I could see it in his face, when he saw how much people enjoyed the films. Those were fun days.

'I tried to be a good boy. Our family went to church regularly. I bought into religion hook, line, and sinker. I served as an altar boy, often read scripture to the congregation, and I fought hard to keep a cap on my sexual curiosity because I was constantly being told that it was a major sin. I even considered attending a theological seminary to become a pastor. I'm truly happy I didn't make that choice.

And then my mother was diagnosed with breast cancer. I vividly remember the afternoon in very early December in 1953, when my mother walked into my dad's office and told my father and me that she had just come from Dr. Paterick's office where they found a lump in her left breast, and they would have to take it out because it might be malignant. That was three days before Christmas, and she said to my dad and me, "I want to wait until January to have the surgery." This news terrified me. We were both way too young for this to happen. I was thirteen, and my mom was thirty-three. That 1953 Christmas had an underlying current of unsureness. Through the family gatherings, neighborhood parties, presents, Christmas dinners, and midnight church services, I kept trying to tell myself it was most likely benign. Little did we know about the difficult journey ahead of us as a family.

She had the surgery, a total mastectomy, the second week of January. Dr. Paterick, who was also our neighbor, was crying when he met with us after the surgery. "She won't have a clean bill of health for five years," he said. "Oh, God no!" I thought to myself. "How can I handle this uncertainty?" I started checking into cancer diagnostic probabilities and found out quickly that my mother's prognosis was probably that she would receive chemotherapy, lose her other breast in about a year or less, and then she'll live maybe another six months.

This was unacceptable for me. My father was frozen with worry and fear, so I took it upon myself to research everything medically going on in the field of breast cancer research, looking for some other options for her. I heard about Dr. Manheimer, a highly respected woman oncologist at the University of Texas, MD Anderson Cancer Center in Houston who was doing groundbreaking work in breast cancer. I remember reading that Dr. Manheimer said she'd never lost a patient. That was exactly what I needed to hear, even though it was an outright lie. I talked to my parents about her and told them what I had learned and convinced them to meet with her.

We drove to Houston and met with Dr. Manheimer, and Mom was accepted as a patient. That started a fairly regular 200-mile trip, driving from San Antonio to Houston and back. As time wore on, there were many times I said to myself, "Why did I do that? Did I just prolong my mother's pain?" I used to kneel when I went to bed at night, I would pray and pray and pray to God, to find a way to save her. I shared a room with my younger brother, Doug, and through the wall we could hear her coughing throughout the night when the fluid was filling up in her lungs. We would carry her to the backseat of the car and drive her back to Houston, sometimes in the middle of the night. So, it was back and forth. Maybe I made her life and our lives more difficult by trying to do something against the odds, which were extremely poor when you had that kind of breast cancer in the 1950s.

It was a tumultuous time. My father didn't know how to handle my mother's illness. One day after her first mastectomy, I overheard him in the bedroom saying, "You've only got one of what most women have two of." It was almost as if cruelty was the only way he could express his pain. Her sickness wreaked havoc on his life. I think he felt completely helpless watching his wife suffer and slowly die. Not to mention the worry of caring for three kids, especially my little sister, Terrye, who was only seven.

Mom was very sick when I entered college. I was barely seventeen years old because I had skipped the fourth grade. I wanted to be close to her, so I enrolled in Texas Lutheran University in Seguin, Texas, just a few miles away from our home in San Antonio. She died a year later when she was just thirty-seven. I remember how difficult it was to wake my sister in the middle of the night to tell her that her Mommie had gone to heaven.

Unfortunately, my family never sat down and talked about my mother's death. We never held each other or even held hands or prayed together or shared our grief with one another. That was just the way my father had been raised. It was more or less the Germanic heritage that ran through the roots of our family, plus my dad's hard upbringing, losing his mother and father by the time he was twelve. We just gritted our teeth, and kept going, and dealt with life and our sorrow in whatever way we could.

The death of my mother triggered a re-examination of my life. Suddenly, I began to question everything, especially religion. I had to accept that I would not be able to control everything in my life the way I had imagined. Time was not endless and not reversible. Do what you want to do while you can. Don't worry so much about doing the right thing; just do want you are passionate about. Don't overthink everything, and if you fail, learn from your failures.

After my mother's funeral, I transferred to the University of Texas in Austin.

ON LOCATION IN SAUDI ARABIA
SEEING NEW WORLDS THROUGH THE LENS
OF TELEVISION

The route from being an aspiring young director in Texas to making your own shows on national television doesn't often go through Saudi Arabia but mine did, a place I'd never been and knew little about. Before I went to the Middle East, I'd never been out of the country except for Mexico.

I was still living in Texas, had just gotten my master's degree at the University of Texas, and was working full time at the small Public Television Station for Austin and San Antonio, KRLN, which broadcast from the UT campus itself. I was wet behind the ears but I was asked to teach a freshman class listed as "Introduction to Television." Having little actual TV experience, I had to work overtime to come up with three forty-five-minute lectures every week for my students, many of whom knew as much about television as I did. I didn't even know yet that television would become the focal point of my career for six decades.

There was an Arabian student in my class named Saleh Mozanni, and we became friends. My buddies at KRLN and I, along with Saleh, would often play poker or go fishing and enjoyed spending time together. However, when we went fishing it was imperative that Saleh bring home fresh fish to his wife. If he didn't bring home fish, he would be humiliated in the eyes of his wife. Since we weren't great fishermen, often we left Lake Travis in Austin empty-handed. But Saleh never went home empty handed. We would always laugh as Saleh stopped at the fish market on the way home.

Saleh left college and went back to Dhahran, Saudi Arabia in 1964, where King Faisal made him the head of television for the entire country. We lost touch, but six months later, Saleh wrote to me, asking if I'd come over and help him set up a television network and help them create television programs. They had money, but no know-how, and the cultural rules were very strict. The conservative Islamic Mullahs feared that too much Western influence would be brought into the country with television, and they wanted to stop it. Saleh had hired RCA Television to set up a studio, television towers, and an entire broadcasting system, but their engineers were often the target of snipers. Two of them had been killed while working high up on a broadcasting tower in Riyadh.

Despite what seemed like impossible, even dangerous circumstances, I was thrilled by the chance of this fascinating adventure, a land and culture completely outside anything I'd ever seen or experienced. Saleh made me an offer I couldn't refuse—seventeen thousand non-taxable dollars for one year. That was extremely big money in 1964, especially for a guy in his early twenties.

He would also pay all the travel and living expenses for me and my first wife, Beverly. We would live at the Arabian-American Oil Company (Aramco) compound on the shore of the Persian Gulf near Dhahran. In exchange, I asked for something I really wanted—the chance to make a serious documentary while I was there.

When I arrived, Saleh was still having difficulty getting the conservative religious leaders to accept television. This seemed like an insurmountable problem, but it was my introduction to figuring out ways to get around cultural limits. If you let the insurmountable stop you, you'll never make a show.

I suggested we put the Islamic Mullahs on television. How could they refuse that? Five times every day all Arabs face Mecca, the holy city of Islam, and pray. Why not put the Mullahs on television five times a day leading those prayers. It seemed like a small thing, but it worked. It was a major cultural change for Saudi Arabia, and television was no longer the enemy.

However, I had no idea of how pervasive the restrictions were not just for television but for how life was lived. Saudi Arabia felt to me like it was living far back in time. Donkeys and camels were the mode of transportation, cities in the desert had one well where everyone came for water, and women, always veiled, still carried things in baskets balanced on their heads, and were barely acknowledged.

It was here that I began to understand that television programs could be more than news and entertainment, that they could be a source of helping people by teaching them simple things like running their homes, or how to make their lives more productive. Women were rather isolated, nearly invisible in this highly patriarchal society, and there was a lot they were curious about, wanted to learn, if we could reach them.

I began to come up with ideas for shows, but there was still this insurmountable problem of never showing a women's unveiled face. Only husbands, parents, or brothers and sisters were allowed to see the unveiled face of the women in their family. I knew that without some personal connection to the person on screen, the program feels cold and impersonal, and the audience gets quickly bored. How could we come up with a way to feel a connection with the women on screen? I thought, why not shoot over their shoulder, so you don't see their face, but you hear their voice, watch their hands and how they inter-act with others. A sense of their personalities. The first show we put together was called *Albayt Alsaeid* or *Happy Home*. Using that over-the-shoulder technique, we showed women washing vegetables, cooking certain dishes, bathing their babies, and changing diapers, all in the interest of improving hygiene, and creating a home while protecting loved ones from infections. And by hearing them talk and watching them work, we felt we were getting to know them as people. Saleh and I felt we these were the first steps in giving women a presence, addressing their lives, and helping them solve problems. Tiny seeds perhaps, but television could now be seen there to enrich their lives, not harm it. It taught me too the wider value that programs could have, and that no problem should stop you from trying. The bigger the problem, the more you must look for new solutions.

We also produced a fun quiz show called *Al'Asyilat Laha Iijabat* (*Questions Have Answers*). And of course, five times a day we would interrupt our programming for prayers that were led by Islamic Mullahs.

We felt we were making inroads in creating the country's first network, lessening the clergy's fears about television, and contributing something to the country. I was getting real hands-on experience as a director and producer, and six months into my stay, I was eager to start on something I'd always wanted to do—make a full-scale documentary. My subject was the ancient Arab civilization, the Nabataeans, who lived in Saudi Arabia around 400 BC, and who historian Jane Taylor has called "one of the most gifted peoples of the ancient world." They controlled trade routes from Europe across Arabia to India and the Far East, and their story was a historical puzzle which fascinated me. The Nabataeans were traders who lived in grass huts, built a sophisticated irrigation system, and carved elaborate tombs out of the rock outcrops in the middle of the desert. They also built the magnificent city of Petra out of the red sandstone in what is now Jordan.

My destination was a valley in the northwest part of the country that the Nabataeans occupied for two centuries. It had become a place of legend called Mada'in Saleh. When the Prophet Mohammed traveled in 600 A.D. through this valley, he saw human bones buried in what looked like carved rocky homes. In the Koran, Mohammed talks about a civilization of evil people who were struck dead in their houses by Allah. In the 1960s and even today, the Mada'in Saleh is considered to be haunted, and while Arab travelers will pass through, often in caravans of camels, they would never spend the night there, claiming they can hear the crying voices of children echoing through the mountains.

To get there, the insurmountable problem was that we'd have to pass through the two most sacred cities in Islam—Mecca and Medina—and not being a Muslim, I was not allowed to enter either city. If I were caught as an "infidel," the punishment was death. I was scared, but thought, well, we'll have to figure something out.

I knew that the country as a whole was distrustful of Westerners, but I found in my personal relationships that my Arab colleagues were warm and outgoing, especially when they saw how interested I was in learning about them and their culture. I enjoyed hearing their stories, going to their villages, drinking tea together, wearing the same red and white head scarf, the keffiyeh, and sharing a meal. Perhaps that is why I was so eager to make the documentary and travel through the country. I find that if we have a sincere interest in one another, and treat each other with respect, we can get along with anyone. This attitude has served me in good stead through the years, and it certainly served me well there, where we had many problems to get around, but did so, together as a team.

We flew on a DC-3 to Jeddah on the Red Sea and were met by our twelve-man crew and two large trucks. A representative of the government, Abdulla Salih Hadlak, joined us to ensure we did not remove any ancient artifacts. I remember so many faces and names—our driver

Mohammed, a production assistant Ahmed Abu Aysha, and the direc-tor of photography, Jack Madvo, who was from Lebanon and bilingual and who helped me translate through the trip.

Our first task was to smuggle me through these cities. I'm obviously not Arab, and I'm also quite tall and not that easy to hide. When we got to the outskirts of Mecca, we pulled off the road, I climbed into the back of our truck, curled up as best I could, and was covered with boxes of supplies and a tarp. As we passed through Mecca and Medina, I was tempted to sneak a peek from under the tarp but didn't have the guts to do it. Besides, it would have gotten my colleagues into terrible trouble.

When we finally reached Mada'in Saleh, we emptied out our supplies, and bought four sheep which we would butcher during our two weeks of shooting. During the shooting, we explored and photographed the tombs themselves, the irrigation systems, and the layout of the valley. During the day it got quite warm, but at night it was always cold. One of our trucks got stuck in the sand, and we all grabbed shovels to get it moving again. I remember one particular incident where, with my crew, I negotiated with a caravan of camels and sheep that was mov-ing through the valley. As is the custom, we sat down, had a cup of tea, and negotiated an agreement with the caravan leader. We would pay him fifty Saudi riyals to go through the valley three times.

We shot the first pass and felt good about it but needed to shoot more footage. We waited ... waited ... and then learned that after the first pass the caravan just kept moving South. At that point, Moham-mad got in the truck, caught up with the caravan and said, "You have to come back through the valley two more times for us". Mohammad said it was a difficult negotiation, and we had to kick in twenty-five more riyals. But they did return and made two additional passes through the valley. And that is the way it works making movies in the middle of the desert in Saudi Arabia. Through the years I found that Hollywood sometimes works that way too.

Traveling in the wilderness, the long stretches of sand and desert, the dark night sky full of stars, the ancient myths filling the air, the sheep we cooked for dinner, were all thrilling experiences, especially for a young, untraveled man like me.But what I remember most was the camaraderie that developed among us. I was the only Westerner in this group, but I never felt alone or outnumbered. We began as strangers from different cultures, but we built ties of connection and respect.

As a team we were all professionals, and figured out how to work with one another, to share information and solve problems together, and emerged as friends. Directing this documentary reaffirmed my passion for telling stories and creating emotional moments. I will always be grateful to Saleh Mozanni and Aramco for underwriting this remarkable adventure, one of the first steps I took as a director and into the world beyond Texas. The documentary, *Valley of Saleh*, was first seen on Saudi Arabian television in 1965. I was told that it was also shown extensively in the Middle East. Aramco owned the picture, but to the best of my knowledge never tried to market it or share it in any way. At times I've wondered if they hid the negative master in one of the Nabataean tombs.

BACK IN THE USA

In 1967, after returning from Saudi Arabia, I wanted to get a job that would help me get more experience in directing television. Fortunately, I had passed the State Department test for the Foreign Service when I was in graduate school at Texas. That helped me land a dream job with the US Information agency in Washington. There, I directed numerous soft propaganda pieces that were supplied free to nations around the world. I got to work with Diana Ross and the Supremes on her success story that aired all across Africa. We sent Carlos Santana performances to South America, and performances of dozens of other artists to countries around the world ... artists who had succeeded because they lived in the USA. These were soft propaganda pieces for American democracy. Propaganda or not, my experience in directing these popular artists was just what I needed! I was building confidence within myself and working with a wide range of artists. Truth is, I would have paid them for those opportunities.

But you can't work in Washington without getting involved in politics. Charles Guggenheim, an Oscar-winning documentarian, offered me a job working at his company producing and directing political spots for various Democratic candidates. I loved politics and had volunteered my time working on numerous political campaigns even when at the University of Texas including the 1960 presidential campaign where I worked for LBJ and a young senator from Massachusetts I grew to believe in, John F. Kennedy. The '60s were turbulent times, especially 1968. I was disillusioned as my country struggled with Vietnam and the civil rights movement, and when in a few short months both Martin Luther King and Robert Kennedy were assassinated. I felt like I'd been hit with a truck. After Bobby Kennedy's assassination, our efforts switched to Hubert Humphrey, not as charismatic a leader as Bobby Kennedy, but I felt much better about him than Richard Nixon, the Republican candidate. Working with Bob Squier and Guggenheim, I was at the 1968 Democratic Convention in Chicago with its political turbulence inside the arena, and riots outside with thousands of anti-Vietnam protesters, who battled with Chicago cops sent by Mayor Richard Daley, one of the last big city bosses in America. Havoc was all around us. Every night I walked home through massive civil unrest in the park, thankful that I got through the violence and into my hotel room safely. While in Chicago, I met Al Perlmutter, who was covering the convention for NBC news. Our paths would cross again soon.

MAKING TELEVISION DANCE
THINKING OUT OF THE BOX

In 1971, I took a leap and left the world I knew of traditional and political documentaries to join the most freewheeling, creative, and experimental place in television. It was the riskiest, most liberating thing I'd ever done. Here was a brand-new program, where if you could imagine something, you could try it, and I had the chance to be part of it. To play in the creative sandbox of the fledging public television station in New York, WNET. I hadn't expected the call, but when it came, I jumped at the chance.

So my first wife Beverly and I, along with our three-year old daughter Jennifer, left Washington where I'd been working with the Oscar-winning documentary film producer Charles Guggenheim, a man from whom I had learned so much, and set out for New York City, and the uncharted waters of non-commercial television. The job was to direct the second season of the very cool, very irreverent program called *The Great American Dream Machine*.

The producer who called me, Al Perlmutter, was someone I'd met four years earlier when we'd each been covering the firestorm of the 1968 Democratic political convention in Chicago—he for NBC and me for Bob Squier, a top political consultant who had worked on the presidential campaign for Hubert Humphrey. By this time, I felt I was in a rut working exclusively on political campaigns. Al had left the networks, which he felt where driven by numbers, to produce several programs at WNET (PBS Channel 13 in New York), a place Perlmutter described as being driven by ideas. Their mandate, he told me, was to create alternatives to network programs, to try new things, even if that meant failing sometimes. I thought, wow, someone understands you can't find out what's possible unless you're willing to go down a few wrong roads. I couldn't wait.

I knew my way around video. I felt comfortable and confident with the new tools, which by today's standards are cumbersome, heavy, and rudimentary, but back then were the cutting edge. This program would give me the chance to explore ways to use the medium, and find out what it could do, how it could work with or shape or enhance the way things are presented in surprising new ways. I'd be working with some of the freshest talents around, on the staff and on the show. Artists I loved, songwriters and dancers, humorists, journalists, novelists, actors, and documentary makers.

WNET rented us a beautiful apartment on Central Park South, smack dab in the heart of New York, steps away from Central Park, 5th Avenue, Broadway and FAO Schwartz, six floors of the classiest toy store I ever walked into. A far cry from our house in Washington's sedate Capitol Hill.

The apartment had deep green velvet walls, Italian marble with lots of brass trim, dozens of books, and a large picture of Frank Sinatra in the living room. After flipping through some books, it became obvious that we were subletting Mario Puzo's apartment, the man whose book, *The Godfather*, had come out two years earlier. Now we were cooking in his kitchen. Not bad for our first apartment in New York. I just hoped we didn't find a horse's head in our bed.

The program I had come to direct, *The Great American Dream Machine*, was a much talked-about show, but so different from other programs that people didn't know how to describe it. It was a fast-paced, satirical but sometimes serious magazine show with no host,

Television comes to San Antonio, 1949

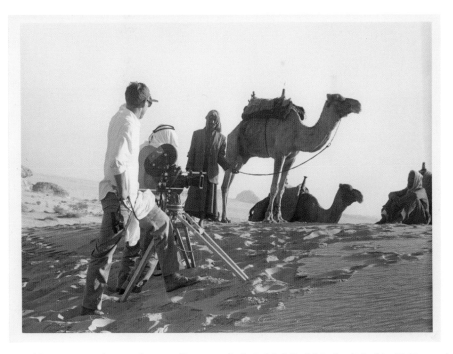

Negotiating with a camel caravan for a second take in Mada'in Saleh, Saudi Arabia, 1965

Taking a break and escaping the brutal sun in the Saudi Arabian desert, 1964

Don directing camera closeup of Mikhail Baryshnikov for PBS's *Baryshnikov by Tharp,* 1985

Discussing a scene with Barbara Walters and President Reagan in his Jeep at his ranch, 1984

Don and Willie talk details about an upcoming shoot with Willie floating down the Rio Grande, 1987

Michael Jackson's 1993 Superbowl Halftime Show which changed Superbowl
Halftime Shows forever, according to the New York Times.

Two of Don's favorite people

The garbage room underneath Atlanta's Olympic Stadium where secret meetings were held with Muhammad Ali's team to keep his appearance a surprise, 1996.

Rehearsing with Ali in a secret 3am rehearsal in Atlanta's blacked out Olympic Stadium, 1996

Despite his Parkinson's Disease, The Champ still exuded nobility, stature and respect
at Atlanta Olympics, 1996

"Summertime and the Livin' is Easy" from Atlanta Centennial Olympic
Games Opening Ceremonies, 1996

Some much needed quiet time with wife, Suzan

A five story high Junk, with sailors working on the masts, travels through the seas in Shanghai's Special Olympics Opening Ceremonies

Prince in the rain! "Best Superbowl Halftime Ever." New York Times. 2007

Torn 9/11 Flag from the World Trade Center carried into Olympic Stadium in hushed silence, Salt Lake City 2002

Don's team, rehearsing Barack Obama's Inaugural Concert at The Lincoln Memorial, 2009

President Obama and First Lady Michelle Obama at the Inaugural Concert
in Washington DC, 2009

Last minute notes with Bruce Springsteen before the Superbowl XLIII
Halftime Show Rehearsal, 2009

Working out Tom Hanks' entrance on the Oscars stage, 2012

Don celebrates getting a 3 hour live broadcast off the air on the second!

Cover of Directors Guild of America Quarterly Magazine, 2013

The West Point Glee Club salute's surviving Tuskegee Airmen at the opening of the Smithsonian's National Museum of African American History, 2016

Quincy Jones presents Don the Director's Guild of America's Lifetime Achievement Award, 2018

and many different segments that took on a wide range of subjects in a variety of styles—mini docs, sketch comedy, investigative reporting, dramatic pieces, songs, and animation. The concept was you didn't know which segment would come up next, so you never knew what to expect.

Everyone in town wanted to appear on a segment, including many new faces—Andy Rooney, Chevy Chase, Penny Marshall, Albert Brooks. Henry Winkler, Studs Terkel, Faye Dunaway, and Don McLean with his new song, "American Pie," that I told him was too long and would never play. Luckily, he didn't listen to me.

One minute I was working with Blood, Sweat, and Tears, and the next with Kurt Vonnegut, then an amazing young Black dancer, Mathew Rushing from the Alvin Ailey Dance company. We did one show just about death and ended it with our tongue-in-cheek humorist Marshall Efron's six-word soliloquy on the question, "Is there sex after death? No!" and the screen faded to black.

It was a mind opener for me. It triggered me to think in a much more creative way. Out of the box...no limits...try anything and everything, and not be too embarrassed if some things didn't work. We aimed largely at young people (and were years before *Saturday Night Live*) but really anyone interested in seeing things in different ways. The show was meant to surprise, shock, amuse, entertain, and jiggle the mind.

I was having a great time; the show really kept me on my toes. It taught me to work under tight time constraints, partner with artists from every field and always stay ahead of things. I had to do a lot of homework and came home to our apartment exhausted. And exhilarated.

Despite the show's popularity—*TIME* magazine called it one of the top ten programs of the year—*The Great American Dream*

Machine was canceled after my season. Our take on the news and comments about the war in Vietnam so irritated the right-wing politicians in Washington, that President Nixon's Director of Communications put pressure on the National Endowment for the Arts to stop funding WNET, so PBS had to end our show. But it didn't end my connection with the pioneers of television. Another call would come a few years later.

I'd gotten a reputation at WNET as a TV director interested in experimenting and putting in time with artists. So, in 1977, when Twyla Tharp, dance's brightest young rebel choreographer, wanted to do a dance program for PBS, she called me.

Her idea was to explore every new way that video had not been tried before to show dance—all sorts of new aspects from how close we could shoot (even eyelashes!) to how many dance images could be made, held, or overlapped on screen. How could television enhance how dance was experienced through the screen, and at the same time, how could dance teach TV a few new tricks? I was game to try it all, inside and outside the studio.

At the time, most TV directors had been little more than video technicians, people who ran the cameras and the control room and made sure things got recorded without too many glitches. Slowly, things had started to change and while most directors still just went straight into the director's booth and looked at the monitors, I didn't like being isolated up there and giving directions with "voice of god" announcements booming through the studio. I decided to work on the studio floor with a rolling cart of camera monitors. Now I could be just a few feet away from the performers—looking at them eye to eye, giving them quiet notes, asking to move their shoulders, feet, torso, or head to position them perfectly for the camera shot. It gave them confidence and I felt the adrenalin of being part of the creative process. I'd study a piece. be it a song, dance, or sketch, until I knew it all by heart, which allowed me to focus on camera moves and angles and really work with the performers, not just cover them. Plus, I knew my way around the new technology.

I couldn't dance, but I knew music and marked my camera shots on the musical scores. I'd memorize every step that happened so I knew where I could cut or push in or go for a close-up. I'd be out there with Twyla as she came up with wacky and wonderful things to try, as we used the full deck of video tools and toys we had to play with. She was a rule breaker, and I was learning from the best. We fell on our faces a lot, but we kept going, and that turned out to be another great lesson. Your most interesting work can come out of your mistakes.

The NEA grant we had gotten to do *Making Television Dance* stipulated that we have a black-and-white documentary team follow us constantly to document the process. Despite our efforts, we didn't produce a show that came close to the artistic imagery we were hoping for—while the black-and-white documentary had become more interesting than the show itself. This documentation of our glorious failure became the backbone of what turned into an award-winning PBS program also called *Making Television Dance*, which is still shown and studied about innovations in early TV.

The documentary included some of the rehearsal footage I'd shot with Twyla when she created her second dance with Mikhail Baryshnikov. They had allowed me to film them—no holds barred—as they worked, and the dance took shape. I even filmed Misha watching Twyla as she demonstrated movements to him for the first time. Something never seen before on television.

Misha was the most thrilling dancer of our time and had recently defected from the Soviet Union where they only allowed him to dance classical ballet. As an artist with a real hunger to try all kinds of dance, those restrictions felt to him like he was being starved for air. After he came to the US, his first non-classical new dance was with Twyla, resulting in the groundbreaking piece "Push Comes to Shove," a huge hit filled with exuberant dancing and derby hats set to ragtime and Haydn. It changed Baryshnikov's image and direction and would be part of a program I later made with them both for PBS.

This second dance, which we filmed in rehearsals, was set to the music of Frank Sinatra. It was called "Sinatra Suite" and became another signature hit. We later filmed Misha performing it on stage with Elaine Kudo from the American Ballet Theater. It was one of three dances, along with "Push Comes to Shove" and "The Little Ballet," in the program we made together for PBS called, *Baryshnikov by Tharp.*

I remember being amazed, as I watched Misha dance, because while many dancers make their moves with blank faces and seem to have dance counts bouncing back and forth in their mind, when he danced, he used every part of his body—especially his face and eyebrows, always with a twinkle in his eyes.

When you're in the midst of working on these shows, totally focused on every detail and decision and idea, you don't really appreciate how creative the atmosphere is, and this one just tingled with electricity, a daring and dynamic exploration across the entire dance spectrum. Then I look back and can't believe how lucky I was to be there and a part of it.

When we worked together, whether on experiments or rehearsals or the performances, I did my homework, and knew every inch of the score, memorizing every step as they worked on a piece. I stayed out on the floor with them, following closely as they tried one thing and then another. Sometimes I'd suggest a way they might move so I could better capture it with a camera, and a few times they even listened to me.

Misha's English was still a bit rudimentary, but we easily communicated through the music and the choreography. I could see how blown away he was when I demonstrated his moves to the camera people so they could see where and how I wanted them to frame their shots. Not always head to toe, as they used to do it. Sometimes a close-up of his face or feet. Another rule broken. Misha laughed hysterically when I tried to imitate his leaps. We all did. I still have it in our blooper reel. I stayed on the floor during the final taping, watching things on the rolling monitors, which was also something new in TV.

Those were my last shows during those pioneering days at WNET 13, although I returned many years later to do a *Great Performances Tap Dance in America* special with the great and much missed Gregory Hines. It was the first *PBS: Great Performances* program dedicated totally to tap dancing.

I have remained good friends with my rule-breaking teacher, Twyla Tharp. As with Misha. By 1982, he had become famous and adored in America and asked me to direct him in a one- hour network special for CBS called *Baryshnikov in Hollywood*. Maybe because he had enjoyed watching me try to imitate him or because we'd developed a trust together of trying new things, in this show, we had him dance in places where he'd never danced before—all over Universal's back lot, on the sets of *Jaws, King Kong,* as well as on a Mississippi riverboat. Most spectacularly, he danced on top of the Universal tram, jumping from the roof of one car to the other while the tram was carrying tourists around on the back lot tour. It was a wonderful reminder of the times I'd worked and experimented at WNET. You see, you never forget the people who encouraged you to try new things, to go out on the high wire of the new. Making art, making friends, making yourself better. Making television dance.

WHEN THINGS WENT WRONG
FAILURE IS A GREAT TEACHER

By 1975, I was living in New York with my wife and two young children in a small apartment on 74th Street. Most of my work was for public television with occasional low budget and hardly watched late night TV specials and instructional videos. I was still dreaming about directing high profile and high budget primetime television. I was struggling, not sure about how to get there, but then I got a break. Or at least I thought so.

Lorne Michaels, a young comedy writer and producer, asked me to direct a new late night show he was creating called *Saturday Night Live* on NBC. He described it as hip and young, a show I knew I'd like to do. Then, Roone Arledge, the brilliant producer and game changer at ABC Sports, asked me to direct his new show, *Saturday Night Live with Howard Cosell*, on ABC primetime. Either show could be a great opportunity, but I had a family and my future to think about and went with the Cosell show. It was high profile, prime time with a famous host vs another late night with unknowns, a much larger paycheck, a guarantee of eighteen episodes, and probably an entrance into big time network specials. Roone Arledge was a legend in news and sports. A big thinker who had created the *Wide World of Sports, Monday Night Football*, and personalized Summer and Winter Olympic Games with emotional stories about the athletes, the "thrill of victory and the agony of defeat." Besides everything else, I'd be working with

THE one and only Roone Arledge, someone I'd always admired. It felt like this was a sure thing, all the way round.

I had wanted this show to be perfect, which would mean booking acts early enough so I could build special scenery, design unique staging, explore dramatic camera angles, and create great transitions from act to act. But that was never going to happen, not with the producers who by and large came from the world of sports. They were fabulous at what they did, which meant filming whatever action was happening at the moment it was happening—more or less just winging it. Their job was to cover existing events, not create them. But variety shows are entirely created. There is just an empty stage until producers put something on it and directors comes up with ideas to make them work.

Saturday Night Live with Howard Cosell would air Saturdays from 8:00 to 9:00 PM. The first show on Sept 20th, 1975, had a powerhouse line up—Frank Sinatra, Shirley Bassey, John Denver, Billy Crystal, and to kick it off, I had the cast of Broadway's *The Wiz* march up Seventh Avenue and into the old Ed Sullivan Theater at 53rd Street, down the aisle to end with a big finish on stage. *TV Guide* wrote, "Despite big-name guests, *Saturday Night Live with Howard Cosell* was pretty much dead-on arrival, with a cringingly awkward host." Cosell knew his sports but not much about the world of entertainment.

We would often meet in his office on Sixth Avenue, then take a break and walk around the block. He called me, "Misch," and I think he loved walking around the block because he was always besieged by adoring fans. Several times Howard said, "Misch, your job is to protect me. People expect me to tell it like it is—to level with them—to tell the truth!" Howard was a good soul. People loved him. I was always impressed with his straight-forward, honest relationship with Mohammed Ali. But he fell to introducing our show's performers, many of whom he didn't know, as though they were sports figures on the playing field, calling many of them, "the greatest of all time."

Our first show had been booked in advance because the Sunday supplements of every newspaper's entertainment section and *TV Guide* wanted to put the show and Howard on their cover. ABC was heavily promoting the show and loved having a big-name line up.

After that first show, Roone and Howard started booking the Saturday night show on Thursday, two days before air.

Every week, we "scrambled" to pull everything together. There were times when we were counting down to go live, and I didn't even know how we would end the show. While we on the air, acts got switched, and the running order changed, making it nearly impossible for me as the director and my team to keep up. It was like trying to direct rush hour traffic with no one obeying the traffic signals.

On one particular Saturday night, we had finished our dress rehearsal, and had about fifty-five minutes before air. I was working on my script to nail down loose ends. Roone was reading the paper in the back of the control room when I heard him say, "Oh! Lionel Hampton is in town." Perhaps you can imagine what came next. He contacted Lionel, booked him, got vibraphones sent over, and rushed Lionel over to the 53rd Street Theater to do a quick mic check. By that time, we were seconds from air, and when I cued Howard to introduce him, I had no idea what Lionel Hampton was performing, how long it was, or what the tunes were. These last-minute changes, common in sports, cause complete confusion on a live variety show that has to be off the air exactly at 9:00 PM and not one second later.

The first show had respectable ratings, but not enough to call it a hit. After that, the ratings went downhill week after week after week. All of this on the first high-profile network television show that I ever directed. As the ratings dropped, we tried desperately to make the show better, including airing Johnny Cash singing his "Train Medley" live from the Texas State Fair Grounds in Dallas. We booked the Bay City Rollers, a hot band from Ireland, and put them on the air live. On the fourth show, we went live to Sea World in San Diego to cover Shamu doing his spectacular jumps and tricks. We were running long and afraid we might get cut off the air before Shamu's biggest jump, and I remember Roone yelling in the control room, "Cue Shamu to speed it up!" I wasn't clear how I was supposed to make an orca, in the middle of his underwater act, go faster, while I sat in my control room on West 53rd Street in Manhattan. Roone wasn't kidding, either. And I wasn't laughing.

The Cosell show, with its guarantee of eighteen weeks, was canceled after eight, and today lives on as one of the biggest bombs in the history of television. I was absolutely distraught when the show ended. I assumed I had blown my one shot and would be forever associated with a show that is still called, "one of the 100 dumbest events in television history."

The stories of what went on behind the scenes with that show began to drift through the industry. About a month later, I had a visit from George Schlatter who had created the original and highly successful Laugh In for NBC. His name was gold in the industry. I couldn't imagine why he would want to meet with a director who had just directed one of the worst shows in television. George said to me, "Anyone who could work with those nuts on Cosell could handle anything. I want you to come to California, bring your family and direct a new version of Laugh In for me." Which is exactly what I did, directing Schlatter's reboot of Laugh In with a new cast that included Robin Williams. It didn't do as well as we hoped and after two seasons it was canceled but doing that show with George changed my career forever.

It was George who kept encouraging me to get out of the control room high above the studio and get down on the floor with a rolling set of monitors that allowed me to talk directly to talent and get more involved in the creative process. He opened doors for me and hired me to direct a *Goldie Hawn Special*, *Goldie and Liza Together*, *John Denver and the Ladies*, and several specials and pilots.

I loved working with these diverse shows. One month with Goldie, then a show with Baryshnikov and the next month with Willie. I was offered series to direct, but I turned them down because I loved the variety of working with different people on different projects with different experiences and concepts. It stretched me creatively, plus I got to pick and choose what I wanted to do. I found my place in television with artists of all stripes and the top creative teams. All from having the failure of *Saturday Night Live with Howard Cosell*.

It had marked a turning in my career, which ultimately paid off big time for me. An instance of what I call functional failure—a disastrous setback which can make you take a turn you didn't expect, and open doors to a future success you never dreamed of. As long as you keep at it, don't give up, and are lucky enough to have someone come along who says, "if you can survive that mess, I'd like you to come work for me."

George Schlatter's mentorship became a deep friendship that continues today. We still call each other once a week and laugh a lot together. Two alta cockers sharing memories, disasters, and all the things we got to do together. Sometimes we like to say to each other, "Hey, what do these kids know today?"

BARBARA WALTERS AND THE SHAH OF IRAN
A WOMAN JOURNALIST IN A MALE-DOMINATED WORLD

During my years living in New York, I worked with one of the strongest forces in news, a woman who was making tidal waves in that male dominated world. ABC had made a big investment in Barbara Walters. She was hired as the first woman prime time news anchor and paid one million dollars a year—more than any of the men in her business. A lot of newsmen found this hard to accept. Misogynistic displeasure was heaped on Barbara, so ABC decided they better make sure she was successful. She was given a series of interview specials with famous people in movies, television, politics, and in some cases world leaders. We were asked to produce and direct them, and we did. The first show was halfway around the world.

When Barbara Walters and our crew landed at Mehrabad International Airport in Tehran, it was very clear that the capital city of Iran was on edge. We were there to interview the Shah of Iran, Mohammed Reza Pahlavi. The Pahlavi dynasty had been in power in Iran for fifty-three years. It was a secular and authoritarian monarchy. But by 1978, the Shah was facing growing discontent which was about to explode into a full-fledged Islamic Revolution.

As we entered Shah Mohammad Reza Pahlavi's palace compound, we could actually feel the tension all around us—security guards were everywhere carrying machine guns and talking into their sleeves that were equipped with mics. I saw it as a clear sign of impending revolution, and possible, perhaps probable, danger for all of us. Not our usual entry to an interview!

It was in February 1977 when Barbara called with the news she had locked in a major interview in the Middle East. Time was tight, and we scrambled to get visas, tech gear, and our crew together. A few days later we arrived in Iran. We were with her to produce an in-depth piece on Shah Mohammad Reza Pahlavi and his Queen, Farah Pahlavi, for *The Barbara Walters Specials*, a new primetime series of specials picked up by ABC which my company, Don Mischer Productions, was co-producing with Barwall, Barbara's company. I was also directing and more than a little nervous about it.

We stayed at the Tehran Hilton and with David Goldberg, our supervising Producer, spent two days surveying locations in the Shah's twenty-seven-acre compound that included palaces, museums, a helipad for the Shah's two helicopters which he piloted himself, and a state-of-the-art speedway where Shah Pahlavi often raced one of his many sports cars. For gaffers, electricians, and tape operators David hired a twenty-six-man Iranian crew, none of whom spoke English. We got off to a bad start the very first day when the entire Iranian crew—all twenty-six of them—walked onto the set exactly one hour late. What was even stranger—each crew member coming onto the set said exactly the same thing, using exactly the same three English words, "Sorry...auto accident."

"Sorry...auto accident."

"Sorry...auto accident." Twenty-six times! Clearly the Iranian production supervisor had given the crew the wrong call time, so to cover, he quickly taught them three words of English to explain their tardiness to the waiting American producers.

The first set-up was in the Shah's mirrored hall of the Green Palace. It was His Majesty's glittering office—and I mean glittering! The walls and ceilings were made entirely of tiny shards of mirror, set in gold trim, which shimmered like a sparkling mosaic.

On the first day of shooting, Barbara and I left the Tehran Hilton together, and discussed our plan for the day on the way to His Majesty's office in the Green Palace. She seemed very well prepared—actually, she was always well prepared. She was smart. And really did her homework. I reminded Barbara, who had just left NBC's *Today Show*, where she was accustomed to doing her interviews live with very strict time limits: "If you had three-and-a- half minutes to interview Ted Kennedy, you would have to often interrupt the Senator to keep him on subject." I said, "But you don't have to do that with a taped interview—just look them in the eye and let them talk. There's no need to rush to the next question. And remember, if you get lost in your notes—no problem— take whatever time you need to find your place because we can just snip that part out." I also suggested to Barbara that when her guests finish answering her question, just sit quietly for a few seconds...most guests, feeling uncomfortable with the silence, will jump in and give you an even deeper, more revealing story. Barbara got it.

When we arrived at the Shah's office. David had things well in hand. We then worked out a detailed plan for Barbara and the Shah to enter, sit, and have a short interview in this magnificent setting. I said, "Now Barbara, when you and the Shah walk into the room, guide him to this chair because his background and lighting are best for him here. Then you sit over on the green velvet sofa that favors your best side,"—her left side. The Shah arrived. We greeted him. We placed Barbara and His Majesty in the hallway for their entrance into his stunning office. Everything seemed in place.

I began rolling the tape to record. Five seconds later, I called, "Action." Nothing happened. Again, "Action...action!" But the door leading into the office remained shut.

Then a member of the Shah's retinue tiptoes over and whispered in my ear, "His Majesty does not open doors!"

I stopped tape and we decided that an aide would open the door and Barbara would enter first, guide the Shah to his armchair, then walk over and sit on the green sofa. Seems simple enough, doesn't it? What could possibly go wrong?

I rolled tape again, called, "Action," and Barbara entered and walked directly to the armchair and sat in the Shah's seat. Meanwhile Shah Pahlavi just stood there wondering where he should sit. On my private intercom I yelled, "Oh no, that's the wrong seat, dammit, and I told her to go sit on the sofa!" The Shah reacted instantly with a very startled look on his face as if he had heard me. But how could that have happened? I was speaking into my personal headset which only the crew could hear. We quickly discovered an open headset was left on the office floor under Barbara's sofa seat. They had both heard me yelling. The Shah was a bit shaken. He's not accustomed to people yelling around him.

Without missing a beat Barbara said, "You see, Your Majesty, we have dictators in our country, too." Normally, I would have laughed. But to be honest, my stomach was in knots. Here we were, surrounded by armed guards, having just met Iranian Royalty in a country that was kind of terrifying, so laughing was not going to happen.

Later that afternoon, we shot the main interview with Shah Pahlavi and Queen Farah in the library of their private residence. Things were going well. Then Barbara brought up the topic of women, their capabilities, and rights. Now, it is very important to remember that it was 1977, and Barbara had just become the first U.S. woman news anchor in history. Today, she is still lauded as the pioneer for all women journalists. But navigating her way through the male-dominated news business, being the highest paid anchor in television—male or female—at the time, was not a walk in the park. She had to be tough, smart, prepared, empathetic, confident, and seemingly unfazed by any man in the room. And she was remarkable.

The interview was going well, and then Barbara asked the Shah out right, "Do you believe women are equal to men?"

The Shah struggled uncomfortably. "Equal in human rights? Yes, sure."

Barbara continued, "What about equal in intelligence?"

"You can always find an exception. But, but ... where is there a top woman scientist?"

"Madame Curie."

"That's one," the Shah admitted.

"Women have a lot of trouble getting ahead—perhaps because of this point of view, Your Majesty. Do you feel your wife is one of those exceptions? Do you feel your wife can govern as well as a man?"

"I prefer not to answer."

Barbara was relentless and undeterred. The Shah was getting angry, and his Queen embarrassed. You could see Barbara looking at the Shah, and then at his wife, and back at the Shah. The mood was becoming very tense as the Shah knew he was getting cornered. Then Barbara came in for the kill, asking, "Well, Your Majesty, if women are not capable of doing these kinds of jobs, why did you make Queen Farah the Regent of your country, so that she takes over in the event that you die? Are there no good men?"

After a long pause, the Shah finally said, "I can't say. I don't know how she would govern in a crisis."

Barbara turned to Queen Farah. "Say something, Your Majesty. How do you feel when you listen to this?"

Farah, looking up to the ceiling, replied, "What can I say?"

The Shah's face turned very red. He rose out of his seat, ripped off his microphone, glared at Barbara, and walked out of the interview.

The head of the Shah's PR team was standing behind me in the truck. He was very, very nervous. "I have never seen His Majesty this angry," he said. "Never!"

Barbara was shaken by the Shah's abrupt move. I quickly left the truck and dashed into His Majesty's library, being stopped twice by security guards with machine guns who said I was moving too fast. People in the room were just standing there not knowing what to do. Barbara gave me this look that said clearly "I went too far, didn't I?" I was worried that the Shah might refuse to show up for the remaining shoots the next day, or worse, just tell us to pack up and head straight for the airport, or even worse yet, confiscate all our recorded tapes, leaving us to fly home empty-handed.

Just then, Queen Farah approached and reassured us that His Majesty would be fine. She would talk to him later that evening and would make sure that her husband definitely would be on location the next day, and he was. I remember being so struck by both women. Barbara's strength and fearlessness and Queen Farah's graciousness and courage. I'm certain, had men been in control that afternoon, the whole shoot would have fallen apart.

Two days later when we boarded the Iran Air 747 to fly home to New York, we were each handed a gift from the Queen—a kilo of Iran's finest purebred Beluga caviar packed in ice and wrapped in a beautiful Persian hand-woven bag. When *The Barbara Walters Specials* aired that April, it became a headline grabbing interview, a big water cooler moment. Today the interview is on YouTube where it still gets thousands of hits.

Five months later, the Islamic Revolution erupted forcing Shah Mohammad Reza Pahlavi, and Queen Farah, to leave Iran. At sunset on January 16th, 1979, they left the palace for the last time by helicopter, flying out over Tehran—a city they would never see again.

The Shah and Queen Farah sought asylum in Egypt. One year later he was treated for lymphatic cancer in the United States after which he returned to Egypt where he passed away on July 27th, 1980. President Ronald Reagan then informed Queen Farah that she was welcome in the US. She bought a house in Greenwich, Connecticut, and she and Barbara Walters continue to be good friends for many years. Since the Pahlavi dynasty ended, the Islamic revolutionaries have ruled Iran. That continues today—after forty-five years.

THE KENNEDY CENTER HONORS
HOW TO CELEBRATE THE PERFORMING ARTS
IN AMERICA

"I am certain that after the dust of centuries has passed over our cities, we, too, will be remembered not for victories or defeats in battle, but for our contribution to the human spirit."

—John F. Kennedy, 1962

New television traditions must start somewhere. I love being at the starting line.

There is an aura to the Kennedy Center Honors. No matter the Honorees, you feel a delight in celebrating all the performing arts, enjoying the achievements of composers, actors, playwrights, singers, dancers, musicians, choreographers. The evening has a classy elegance and joyful celebration wrapped into one.

However, before there was the aura, there was only a pile of unanswered questions. After all, this kind of show had never been tried on television. How would it be different from other award shows? How would we find the emotions to give the show its special appeal alongside top entertainment from the popular and classical worlds?

The idea began when Roger Stevens, the founding chairman of the Kennedy Center and George Stevens Jr. the founder of the American Film Institute came up the notion of a show that would give lifetime achievement awards to artists across a wide breadth of American culture and celebrate their artistic contributions. An annual event in Washington to be broadcast nationally.

George brought in Nick Vanoff, a veteran Hollywood and New York producer, former dancer on Broadway, and a true showman to help develop the show. Five artists would be chosen, each segment to include a spoken tribute, a short biographical film and live stage performances that showcased their work. In effect, a thank you. The Honorees didn't have to appear on stage, speak, or do anything other than just enjoy the evening, seated together in the box next to the president. The White House agreed to host a reception for the artists before the show, and CBS agreed to air it. The deal was set. The first Kennedy Center Honors would be taped on December 3rd, 1978, in the Opera House at the Kennedy Center, and air on CBS two days later on Tuesday night, December 5th.

Now what the producers needed was a television director to figure out how to take the show from stage to the TV screen.

I was asked to fly to Washington to meet with George and Nick, and I did. I landed at Dulles and went straight to the Opera House. From the get-go, George was adamant that television must have a low profile and that the audience, a mix of high-profile Washington dignitaries, including the president, members of Congress, of the Supreme Court, and top performing artists, would not be aware of cameras, cables, teleprompters, and audience lights. George said, "I'd like them to enjoy the two-hour show and leave without any hint that it was being taped for television."

I understood exactly what George was saying because televising an event can contaminate such a show. Technical elements affect a show's rhythm—cameras moving around the aisles, cutting the length of remarks, orchestras playing off speakers, audiences craning around big cameras, and performers playing to the cameras, not the crowd. On the other hand, how do you make a good television program if you have to pretend, you're not there?

George, Nick, and I spent three hours walking around the empty Opera House discussing the possible placement of cameras, the light levels shining on the audience, and how to film the Honorees in their box. You can't throw a party for someone and not see their face. Their responses were key to the emotions of the evening.

As the television director, I had a professional obligation to deliver the best show possible to CBS. And if I couldn't do that, why was I there? I needed cameras in certain positions off the aisles, to shoot the stage at raked angles for the best shots of dancers, singers, and choirs. It's what gives a performance the texture of being alive rather than the flatness of just being covered. I wanted a camera to capture close ups of performers, and another to shoot the faces of the Honorees and the president and the dignitaries. And what about the audience? How could I convey the electricity of an evening, that special "dialogue" between performers and audience, unless we had a camera there too?

But George remained adamant. I knew I couldn't do a good job with these restrictions, and as I've often said to myself, "If there is no solution, there's no problem." I took a cab back to Dulles and flew home, bummed out, because I knew deep inside that the Kennedy Center Honors could be absolutely wonderful.

A week later, Nick called, "Okay, you can have a camera in the left aisle and one on the right, plus one stage right to cover the Honorees and the president." It wasn't as much as I wanted but it was enough to make me say yes. And we all agree that there would be no teleprompter, no cueing of the audience to applaud, no second takes ever, and no stage waits for changeovers. It had to run like a live theatrical event—seamless!

For all of us, we'd be paving this road as we walked it. A national show about the performing arts. Uppermost in my mind was how to capture the excitement and emotions while trying to remain invisible.

Plus, and as corny as it sounds, we all felt we wanted to live up to these giant artist Honorees, who we admired and adored.

The Sunday night show was preceded by a weekend of events, including a formal dinner hosted by the Secretary of State, several lunches, and brunches. Dancers and singers mixed easily with Cabinet Secretaries and Senators, opera stars with Supreme Court justices. Even Republicans and Democrats talked like friends.

Sunday afternoon, the president welcomed the Honorees and their guests at a White House reception. Then they were taken to the Kennedy Center for the 7:30 show. The gala audience arrived with a heightened sense of anticipation. Once they and the Honorees were in place, I'd cue the president and first lady to enter, and the show would begin with the national anthem.

The first Kennedy Center Honors in 1978 was hosted by Leonard Bernstein who got it off to a glorious start. The audience kept turning around to see how the Honorees were responding to the tributes, films, and sparkle of entertainment. The five Honorees, a mix of ballet, movies, Broadway, and the concert hall, were Marian Anderson, Fred Astaire, George Balanchine, Richard Rodgers, and Arthur Rubinstein. Thanks to the cameras, we could watch their faces, alternately overwhelmed, happy, and touched to the core. Otherwise, however, for me the show was pretty much a train wreck.

Scenic cues were missed. When Edward Villella took his bows after his tribute to George Balanchine, a curtain came down on his head. Aretha Franklin, performing in honor of Marian Anderson, caught her heel in the fringe of the house curtain and almost fell over. We'd never rehearsed with an audience, so we had to keep readjusting the lights on them to get shots of their reactions, without blinding them. The audience surprised us by continually standing up and turning to cheer each Honoree. The multiple standing ovations were wonderful, but when the audience turned to view the presidential box, our lighting was way off.

I had to keep the cameras in the aisles down very low, so the audience could see over them to the stage. It meant the cameramen had to actually sit flat on the floor but remain agile enough to shoot both the stage and then swing around and shoot the audience. As experienced as we all were, we were, in the lingo of the business, winging a good deal of it. It seemed very hot in the truck on show night because we were sweating it out in the mobile unit which was parked on the loading dock.

The curtain came down at 10:20 PM, and George, Nick, and I flew immediately to New York to start editing. We had twenty-eight hours to edit and deliver the show to CBS for Tuesday night's airing. A two-hour TV show is only eighty-four minutes of content, which meant we had to cut thirty-six minutes out of the show. And that's not easy.

We started about 1:30 AM Monday morning, well aware that whatever we did would set the tone, appearance, and mood of the show forever. I was ready to dig in and hustle, but George and Nick wanted to keep trying one option after another. Luckily, they fell asleep, totally exhausted around 3:00 AM, and I shifted into high gear, as the sound of the clock ticked away.

The editor and I worked straight through until Tuesday afternoon and finished with seconds to spare. The first hour of the show was already airing from CBS Master Control on West 57th Street. when I gave the second hour to our production assistant, Joe. He jumped in a cab outside our editing house on East 44th Street and traveled across town to CBS. He made it with twelve minutes to spare. Waiting for Joe to call and say he made it, was the longest twelve minutes of my professional life. Or nearly, until the third year when one of the Honorees disappeared.

Leonard Bernstein was an Honoree along with James Cagney, Agnes de Mille, Lynn Fontanne and Leontyne Price. As I was counting down to start the program at 7:30, Bernstein was nowhere to be found. He'd vanished. President and Mrs. Carter were waiting in the anteroom to enter their box, but I couldn't cue them until all the Honorees were seated. A wave came over me, that I can only describe as close to utter panic.

We had stage managers and escorts frantically looking for Bernstein. While the President waited, I felt like there was an invisible person behind me pushing. Get on with it, no wait, get on with it. It wasn't helpful.

Part of the fun for me of being in the director's chair is the constant flow of adrenalin, the lightning-fast decisions you have to make, but I dodged the bullet that night when Bernstein showed up at 7:45. He wound up being the most vivacious and nearly jumping-out-of-his seat Honoree we'd ever had.

We heard later from his manager, Harry Kraut, that Lenny had dozed off upstairs in the White House. He thought that since Ronald Reagan was soon to be sworn in as President, this might be his last chance to visit the Lincoln bedroom, where he accidentally fell asleep.

It was already clear that what made the Kennedy Center Honors work was more than the speeches and stars. It was the moments that made you truly feel something for the Honoree and their work, and when the Honoree sensed the deep sincerity of the tribute. You work hard to create those moments, but sometimes you find them in the spur of the moment, if you're quick enough to seize them.

That is what happened the second year when we honored Henry Fonda. Alan Alda would give the spoken tribute, and as a young actor who wanted to express his admiration, he said, "For someone who had set the standard we actors reach for, but precious few will ever match."

Following the film, several of Fonda's colleagues told stories of working with him, but his segment was missing something, something other than words. One of Fonda's most famous roles was the idealistic Navy officer in *Mister Roberts* and he himself had been a naval officer in the Pacific, so we asked the US Navy Academy Glee Club to sing "Anchors Aweigh." The 125 men of the choir came to rehearse, and as we stood in the empty Opera House, it felt stiff to me—no spontaneity. I knew how much those men admired Fonda, but we were missing that. What could we do with this large choir to give it a visceral connection to Fonda? Without it, it'd just be a number and an exit.

We came up with a plan that became a tradition for the Honors for decades. After finishing "Anchors Aweigh," one man from the Naval glee club stepped forward and spoke, "Thank you, Mister Roberts," and then saluted Fonda. The choirs on stage did the same, and clearly enjoying the moment, they dropped their formal military pose, by breaking ranks and cutting loose—waving and cheering Fonda wildly in the box in a burst of admiration and respect. On the reprise, they exited up the aisle, waving and saluting Henry Fonda. What we didn't expect was that Fonda, normally a somewhat reserved man, would be so moved by this unexpected display of affection, that he stood up as they passed, wiping his tears, saluting, and waving back.

The audience got into the act, standing, and waving at the box. That personal cheering by the performers at the end of their tributes as the Honoree waved back became a signature of the show. Yes, we broke the usual protocol, but it felt genuine and heartfelt, and it really worked.

As the years went on, the audience came expecting those surprise moments, and we had to keep looking for new ways to surprise them, a lot like finding another needle in the haystack. Sara Lukinson, who made the moving films and was one of the show's writers, was terrific at digging up clues about things that meant something to the Honoree, which led us, when we honored Johnny Carson, to the University of Nebraska.

Carson, the classy king of late-night comedy, a man in the center of show business, had quietly been very generous to his alma mater for years. Everyone there was super proud of their connection to him. Not just in the drama and TV department, but the whole school, including their football team and marching band.

Could we get the Nebraska marching band to the Honors, and would it be too corny or just right? I love marching bands and decided to go for it, hoping I could make it work, even with a very limited rehearsal. The kids agreed to drive all night in school buses and get to Washington Sunday morning. They were real troopers. The drum major said, "We'd do anything for Johnny." I rehearsed them very early Sunday in an empty Opera House before any of the stage lights were turned on. After that rehearsal, I knew what a great surprise this would be for Johnny.

We had invited newsman Ted Koppel, who turned out to be a friend of Carson's and funnier than anyone knew, to give the spoken tribute. Then David Letterman came with his top ten list, and the audience thought they'd laughed and seen the big stars, what more could they do for Carson?

Suddenly, a drum major appeared on stage and blew his whistle. Then a loud shout came from the back of the Opera House, "Go Huskers!" Drums kicked in as I cued the curtain behind the drum major to rise quickly revealing drum majorettes, snare drums and trumpeters marching in from both sides, wearing their Cornhuskers Marching Band uniforms. Carson turned in stunned surprise to his wife, before bursting into a disbelieving smile.

And down the aisles (I loved those aisles) marched more majorettes, trumpet, and cymbal players, joining the others on stage, now overflowing with 120 kids. From the truck, I watched Carson, and for the first time I saw this man, who rarely showed his feelings in public, smiling, laughing, and grinning from ear to ear.

One young man stepped forward, "We came tonight to thank you. You've made us so proud to be Nebraskans. Many people think Midwesterners are pretty square, but how can that be, when the hippest guy in America is from North Fork, Nebraska?"

Carson leaned forward in his seat, clearly enjoying every minute of it, as Doc Severinsen joined the band to play the theme from *The Tonight Show*. It worked like gangbusters, and beyond being a huge and fun surprise, it had clearly touched Carson, and given us an insight into his character and private generosity.

Those kinds of moments were one of the many reasons we all liked coming back to do the show year after year. A camaraderie had developed with this yearly opportunity to work together, in a business where that is rare. We had this chance to rise to our best, with our imaginations and professional know how. Plus, my wife Suzan and I got to sit next to Colin Powell and Madeleine Albright at dinners, enjoy the warmth of the White House receptions, and I talked football with Walter Cronkite and Isaac Stern, which wasn't bad either.

After nine years as the Honors' director, other offers were coming my way to both produce and direct and I left the show. Then five years later, all too suddenly, Nick Vanoff died, and George asked me to come back as his co-producer. We continued to share a similar goal—terrific performances edged by emotional moments that surprised the Honorees, while handling those hair-raising moments that come with a show in front of a live audience.

A few years later, in honoring John Kander and Fred Ebb we decided to use the cast of their Broadway show *Chicago*. I rehearsed them on Friday morning at the Kennedy Center, then put them on the shuttle to New York for their Friday night show.

Then, and this was the tricky part, they had to fly back to Washington after their Sunday matinee. It was always tight. And if the weather was bad, it could be a nail biter. We had a team of people, including a police escort at Reagan National Airport, and once we got word that the cast had landed, we could breathe a little easier.

There was always something that could go wrong with Broadway casts flying down after their Sunday matinee; most casts almost missed their flight and showed up with five minutes to spare, before their cue to go on. There were snowstorms, a shy Honoree lingering in the bathroom, opera singers stuck in Chicago, and emergency substitutions two hours before curtain. Luckily there was no more overnight editing, as the show now aired three weeks later.

Despite all the anxiety and stress, I loved the Kennedy Center Honors and was thrilled to be a part of it. I always thought the mix of popular and classical artists was something else that set the Honors apart. I loved watching classical violinists talk backstage with country guitarists. Broadway dancers compare notes with ballet stars. There was no hierarchy, no distinction among the artists. Something we hoped carried over into the show.

I must confess that one of my best memories was the year Willie Nelson got the Honors. I'd done many shows with Willie, filmed in our mutual home state of Texas, the National Parks, the Olympics, Carnegie Hall and the Angels and Outlaw Tour. I felt like, I know this guy, and exactly the kind of surprise that would blow him away. Then our stage supervisor, John Bradley, told me it was out of the question. "So forget about." I wanted to bring on stage his traveling bus and second home, *Honeysuckle Rose*. It weighed thirty-five tons and John said the bus would absolutely break through the floor and plunge down two levels to the dressing rooms.

I knew the easiest thing to say, was well, if we can't, we can't, but I also knew no idea would ever be as good or mean as much to Willie. I kept thinking there must be way to solve this.

I've worked with a lot of talented people and found the best way to motivate them is with slow but persistent encouragement, asking them to give it a shot and to try to explore things they hadn't thought of before—challenge them so they want to succeed at it.

Just because you're the boss, losing your temper or being condescending is the worst approach. I talked with John and our set designer Bob Keene until they moved from impossible to improbable to maybe. In the end, after many consultations with engineers and the team at the Kennedy Center, they came up with a solution. They would reinforce the stage floor with eight by eight beams, enough to carry the thirty-five tons of *Honeysuckle Rose*. The night of the show, after Lyle Lovett sang one of Willie's songs and the applause died down, there was on nothing stage except the huge red curtain. A loud voice was heard.

"Willie ...?"

Silence

"Willie ...?"

Silence.

Willie shouted back, "Yeah?"

The loud voice called out again, "We brought one of your closest friends to be with you here tonight."

Then a loud air horn goes BONK! BONK! BONK!

The curtain flew out revealing *Honeysuckle Rose*. Willie burst into the biggest grin I'd ever seen. The bus door swung open, and Kris

Kristofferson (the loud voice) got out, and sang a kickass version of "On the Road Again." Willie was over the moon. So was I.

Eventually, I left the Honors, as my company expanded, and we took on more projects. George brought in his son Michael as his new co-producer. Then in 2016, a new team was brought in to produce the show.

It has been eighteen years since I stepped on the Kennedy Center Honors stage, a place of memories and pride, music and dance, films, choirs, marching bands and a hundred plus Honorees wiping away a tear. And a reinforced stage.

I can remember that first year so well, when we weren't sure of anything. Then, after a few years, realizing we were creating something lasting. Each year, I'd get on the plane from Los Angeles to Washington, full of anticipation. What another great group of Honorees. I hope we can do it again.

ON THE ROAD WITH WILLIE NELSON
THE BUS, THE RATTLESNAKES, ROADSIDE JOINTS, AND ALWAYS THE MUSIC

Whenever I go down the list of performers and artists I've worked with— Barbra Streisand and Isaac Stern, Beyoncé and Bruce Springsteen, Michael Jackson and Baryshnikov, Prince and Yo-Yo Ma, and so many others, the name I always come back to talking about is Willie Nelson. Maybe because we both came out of the same Texas soil. Maybe because when I was in junior high school, I played a double-neck fender steel guitar with country bands, and Willie was my idol and inspiration. For me, he was the eyes of Texas.

Then, after we started working together, I realized something else about him—he was always the same Willie, whether he was with us on his Outlaw Tour or at Carnegie Hall, the Olympic Stadium, or a national park. Unpretentious, courteous, honest, and never deceitful, unless he was playing cards or dominos in a truck stop along I-35.

I try, with every star I've worked with, to listen to what they want to do and work with or around that. Even if I might suggest something, you can't twist the arm of an artist to sing or say something they don't want to. Some artists make it hard. They push their weight around and puff up their importance, while others make it easy. Willie was the easiest guy I've ever known. Easy in his self, in his music, singing whatever songs he loved in whatever style he wanted, no matter what it was called. If he was comfortable with what he was singing, he was good to go.

Willie was also easy and prolific as a songwriter, and one of the most naturally gifted artists I've ever known. He once said to me, "Good or bad, I just have to keep writing songs." He's written 337 of them, and twenty-five were number one hits. He could sing on any stage and with anyone. He never made a fuss, as long as he had his bus, his weed, and his music.

Willie and I did a dozen shows together, but the time I like to think about most was when we traveled around Texas together for a month, making a CBS Television Special called *Willie Nelson: Texas Style*. Willie and I decided to build the show around visiting his favorite places and letting the audience see Texas through his eyes. We filmed him drifting down the Rio Grande singing "Down Mexico Way" with jazz guitarist Jackie King. He sang with Ray Charles at a club on Austin's famous 6th Street, including "I Can't Stop Loving You" and "Georgia." He sang with Ray Benson and Asleep at the Wheel at Carl's Corner, a truck stop on I-35 just south of Dallas. Carl's Corner was an infamous truck stop between Dallas and Austin known for its raucous truckers. Carl Cornelius himself had lost two fingers when he was accused of cheating in a card game, and an unhappy gambler planted an ax into the card table.

We filmed Willie and his band playing their annual Fourth of July picnic in Hillsboro, his benefit for Farm Aid. A long-time environmentalist, Willie was a champion of family farms. During the breaks, I ate Texas barbecue in the catering tent with Willie and his band, smacking our lips over that great smoky-sweet taste of home. Unlike most artists, especially famous ones, Willie never demanded artist perks—special catering, certain food or drink, or the biggest dressing room. He came with whatever he needed on his bus and always on time, prepared and ready to work. Which meant we could connect through his music, not through any star filter.

Of all the places we filmed in Texas, Willie's favorite was a town in the middle of nowhere near the big bend of the Rio Grande River, called Lajitas. A one-street town not far from the Mexican border in a spectacular desert setting. Getting there had nearly cost us our lives. When we boarded our twin engine prop plane in Austin, we were warned that the weather was deteriorating rapidly in West Texas. Thermals were rising above the hot desert and thunderstorms were developing in our flight path. An hour after we took off, we hit them. We tried dodging them but eventually had no choice but to fly directly into one. It was scary. My wife, Suzan, and I clutched one another in the two cramped passenger seats like it was our last goodbye. Our plane was being whipped around like a ping-pong ball in a wind tunnel. I kept thinking of Willie, knowing he was sitting on his bus, smoking weed, and singing "On the Road Again." At that moment, Suzan and I wished we were on the road too. Of all my trips and adventures all over the world, planning and executing high profile events, this was the closest I ever came to feeling like I was going to die.

We finally broke through the clouds and turned south toward the Rio Grande, the Mexican Border and Lajitas. But I was still nervous when our pilot Bob, took a Texaco road map and without looking at me, threw it over his shoulder and said, "Don, open this road map up and see if we can find out where the hell we are."

The runway at Lajitas was just a strip of graded gravel, with one windsock at the end of it. No terminal. No fuel tanks. No power. Not even a Porto-potty. The control tower where the pilot radioed to say we were landing was the reception desk at the town's only hotel. As we approached the gravel runway, Bob radioed, ""This is a twin engine Cessna coming in from Austin and we are about to land." The desk clerk answered, "Ok! Good luck!" Willie, of course, would be arriving the next day on his bus—*Honeysuckle Rose*.

We spent the remaining daylight hours surveying locations, with co-producer David Goldberg and several of our crew, along country roads filled with armadillos, tarantulas, scorpions, and giant rattlesnakes. I grew up in Texas with these varmints, so no surprise for me. But David and the guys from Los Angeles were totally freaked out and very jumpy!

The shoot was magical. After we shot Willie and Jackie King drifting down the Rio Grande in a rusty old rowboat singing, "Down Mexico Way," Willie introduced me to the Lajitas Mayor—a goat who ate tin cans, who, like so many Texas politicians, does any stunt to stay in office. After our shoot, I sat with Willie in *Honeysuckle Rose*—and asked him why Lajitas attracted him so much. He said, "I love the desert, I love the stars at night, I love the quietness. And I feel at peace and free down here." I got that because I felt the same in that vast open space of West Texas. There were no fences, no highway road signs, and no gas stations for the next 100 miles. Willie, who loves to surprise you, started talking about a good friend of his with the same name as mine, Walter Mischer. There aren't many Mischers in Texas, and I hadn't even met Walter Mischer. I just knew that after the first Mischers immigrated from Germany to Texas, through Galveston, Walter's side of the family settled in the Houston area, while ours had settled in the farming country around Fayette County. We heard Walter had become a wealthy banker and successful developer, who put his money into meaningful projects.Willie said he and Walter had formed a strong attachment over protecting Lajitas and loved to go down there and hang out together. Willie enjoyed watching my jaw drop open. I felt like all these threads in my life came together in this little rugged town in West Texas, another reason I was glad I hadn't died getting there.

Several days later we were shooting a scene at Mona's Yacht Club, close to Willie's ranch on the west side of Austin. Mona's Yacht Club was a rusty tiny tin shack at the edge of a creek feeding Lake Travis. There were no yachts, no deck, just one rusty old rowboat half under water. Willie liked to hang out at Mona's, play dominoes, drink a few beers, and have an occasional greasy hamburger. Strangers would come in and end up playing dominoes with Willie Nelson! Even if you didn't share a real connection, Willie had a way of making everyone feel like a friend.

Late one evening after we wrapped our shoot at Mona's, Willie offered to drive David and me back to Austin in his Mercedes. I was riding shotgun and David was in the backseat when Willie suggested we stop off for one more drink, remembering a little bar up the road. He pulled his Mercedes in front of a wooden building, a single light hanging down, and wide steps up to a double door entrance. We walked up the wooden steps, opened the unlocked door, and strode in.

A middle-aged man in his underwear was watching the evening news on his recliner, while his wife, in a bathrobe with rollers in her hair, was lounging on the couch. They stared at us in shock, but I could tell from their faces they knew who Willie was. Willie, never one to talk too much, said nothing, while I, always the first to say anything, apologized and said Willie had thought this was a bar. The man, without missing a beat said, "Well, it was, but now it's our home." Reaching behind his chair, the man in his undershorts pulled out a bottle of Jack Daniels. "You guys wanna drink?"

We looked at one another and said to him, "That sounds great."

Another one of my fondest memories of Willie—and one that just bustles with unbelievable stories—involved a shoot at Grand Teton National Park, in Wyoming. The Director of the National Parks Service in Washington asked us to create a four-minute promotional film that would encourage Americans to get more invested in their national parks. I jumped at this opportunity because I love our national parks.

We decided to shoot the piece with the Woody Guthrie's classic, "This Land is Your Land," not in Woody's folk style, but with much slower tempo, an anthem-like feel, with layers of rich harmonies. Willie loved the idea and suggested we shoot his part in Grand Teton National Park, with the stunning Teton peaks in the background. So, I contacted the director of Grand Teton National Park and said, "We'd like to come out there at sunrise with the stunning Teton peaks in the background, and have Willie Nelson sing a part of 'This Land' in your strikingly beautiful park." There was a pause, and she replied, "I'm not sure about that. Willie is a drug addict, isn't he?"

I couldn't believe it. Stunned, I said, "Well, Willie has smoked a little marijuana, like the rest of us in Texas, but this man is an American icon, a friend of Presidents, invited by every administration to perform at the White House since LBJ. He's a hero to farmers and workers and has received the Kennedy Center Honors. How could you possibly turn away someone so significant to America?" I tried hard to hide my frustration, and I waited.

Several weeks later, she called back and said, somewhat reluctantly, "Okay." So, we proceeded, knowing her sensitivity to the image of the America's national parks. I traveled with my crew to Jackson Hole, Wyoming, just inside Grand Teton National Park, early on Sunday, September 4th. What a gorgeous western setting. We worked all day laying dolly track, building a long arm camera jib, and setting the shot to be made at sunrise early the next morning. There was a window of about fifteen-twenty minutes where the light would make the shot magical.

Early the following morning we got Willie out there in his bus, in darkness, and rehearsed the shot in the dark using flashlights. We then returned to the bus. As the first rays of light appeared, I let Willie know that it was time to shoot. At that moment, three National Park Service vehicles drove up and parked right next to Willie's bus. I quickly realized that the park director was paying us a surprise visit, with five rangers in tow. They were all in their handsome dress uniforms— dark green flannel shirts, leather straps across their chests, and those hats. They started walking towards the bus. All this was fine, until Willie, still in the bus with me, said, "Before we shoot, I just have one more thing I gotta do," as he took out a joint and lit it. Jesus Christ, I suddenly thought, if we open the bus door now, they're going to get a whiff. I had to do something ... fast.

"I'll be right back," I said to Willie. Willie's bus driver was a crusty old Texan named Gator. As I ran out of the bus I yelled to Gator, "Open the door, let me out but close it behind me immediately." I slipped out and he shut the door, just in the nick of time. "Hey, guys, welcome! Glad you're here. Let's get a picture of y'all with Willie before we shoot this thing," I said to the rangers. I led them thirty yards away from the bus to a split rail fence with the mountains perfectly framed behind them. I went back to the bus, grabbed Willie, and we took some pictures. I felt that I had dodged a bullet.

Then while the rangers watched, we started shooting—a forty-five-foot jib move across the grass with the Tetons looming in the background. Willie was elegantly sliding into frame as he sang the chorus. As we were getting ready for a second take—Willie was talking to the park rangers while Jake, my gaffer from Idaho, came up to me and said, "Hey, Don, can you do me a favor?" Now remember the park rangers were just a couple of feet away, and that they were worried that Willie was a "drug addict." Jake pulled out a magazine from his back pocket and asked, "You think you could get Willie to sign this for me?" What Jake pulled out of his back pocket was a magazine—*High Times*. The cover featured Willie, and the issue was entitled "Willie on Weed."

I told Jake to put that goddamn magazine back in his pocket and, "Don't take it out until you get back to Idaho." I may have yelled. Never a dull moment.

Many years later, I took my son, Charlie, to see Willie perform at the Hollywood Bowl. It was a sold-out crowd of 17,500 people, and Willie felt as at home there as he did back with that man and his wife drinking a Jack Daniels. I had learned so much from him through the years, about the inner honesty of a true artist, about the high marks of a professional, and their lack of pretension. I also saw how you can never mistake an artist's reserve for a lack of determination. Willie's real interest in and curiosity about folks is what makes him able to connect so easily with everyone and to share his love of music—all the music he had listened to growing up as a poor kid in the small town of Abbott on the plains of central Texas. Back then, his radio brought him the world and its music—country, gospel, jazz, blues and most of all, the voice of Frank Sinatra, who he loves above all other singers.

During his show at the Hollywood Bowl, it hit me how we had both become older and slowed down. His show went well, but he had some difficulty singing out the lyrics, and at one point asked the crowd to sing while he played. That he couldn't sing that well anymore didn't make any difference; everyone still fell under his spell, and of course knew the lyrics to all his songs. I had to hold back my tears, wondering if this would be the last time I would see Willie perform on stage. Afterwards, I took Charlie backstage to say hello, so glad that my son got to meet the man with whom I had shared so much of my career,

I count working with artists and performers part of my lucky journey, from my boyhood in San Antonio to my Los Angeles home full of awards, but more importantly, full of memories. I don't remember the first time I worked with Willie but I do remember he said yes to my many requests, which included Liberty Weekend to mark the one hundredth anniversary of the Statue of Liberty, the Closing Ceremonies of the Salt Lake City Olympic Games soon after 9/11, *Dolly* (the Dolly Parton variety show), that promotional ad for the National Park Service, the Outlaws and Angels tour with Bob Dylan and Keith Richards, singing "Living in the Promiseland,"at the Democratic National Convention, and singing "Blue Skies" at Irving Berlin's *100th Birthday Celebration* at Carnegie Hall. And that unforgettable night we honored him at the Kennedy Center Honors and brought the thirty-five-ton *Honeysuckle Rose* onto the stage of the Opera House.

Willie believed that music breaks through all the divides between folks in the country and the city, Republicans and Democrats, presidents and waitresses, audiences at the Hollywood Bowl and Mona's Yacht club. Singing and writing songs is his way to talk to everyone and comes as naturally to him as eating Texas barbecue. I always hoped that through the shows I produced and directed, through the music and dance and entertainment we showed and the emotions we hoped to touch, that we were bringing people together in a shared moment they could take with them. I will always be grateful to Willie, for being my friend, for lighting up so many of my shows, and helping me, another kid from Texas, remember how music can make us feel at home anywhere, and with everyone.

CUE THE EFFING BALLOONS

Having been a Democrat for my entire life, I was very excited when the Democratic National Committee approached me about co-producing and directing the 2004 National Convention at the FleetCenter (now TD Garden) in Boston. I was recommended and supported by Ricky Kirshner, who has served as an event executive producer for all events of the Democratic Party in America for many years. His partner, Glenn Weiss, directed the television feed that was fed to news outlets around the world. But I was hired to produce the convention and direct the four days of events from my perch high above the center cluster of press, television and sound tech crews, and security teams.

For decades, I was riveted in watching national political conventions on television. To me, they were the heartbeat of American democracy, where people debated issues, hammered out platforms for their candidates, maneuvered through back-room meetings and deals, and hopefully emerged as a unified political party with clear objectives and plans for how to achieve them.

In the 1950s and 1960s Democratic conventions, just like Republican conventions, were raucous debates with backroom deals, promises made for votes, and many power plays. The national conventions began on a Monday, often with no one knowing who would be nominated and four days later, on Thursday, the presidential and vice-presidential nominees would be announced. A viewer never knew what was going to happen next because of the kinds of deals made behind the scenes and the maneuvering to accomplish their goals. But that spontaneity that I felt as a kid growing up in the '50s and '60s has disappeared. To me, modern day conventions seem over produced—staged shows instead of an inside look at the dynamic workings of American democracy. It's now all planned, choreographed, and cued from control centers underneath the stands. So a lot of the fun is missing. As is any real suspense.

When Don Mischer Productions was selected, I wanted to try and create a convention that felt different. Historically brass bands always played at the national political conventions. I can still hear them playing "Happy Days Are Here Again" when the nominee finished his acceptance speech. In terms of music, those conventions I watched growing up sounded like John Phillip Souza had written and arranged everything—big, brassy, boring, with the overall feeling of being pompous and old-fashioned.

So, I decided to hire Steve Jordan, an extremely successful Black drummer and music director who gave us a cool and contemporary sound. Steve played songs from the civil rights and the anti-war movements of the '60s and '70s. Very few, if any artist spoke truth to power better than the late great Curtis Mayfield, who was born and raised in Chicago. Steve played on our future Black President with "Keep on Pushing," the Mayfield composition recorded and made famous by the Impressions.

Steve later told me that while Obama was delivering his keynote address, it became very clear to the entire band that he would eventually become president of the United States. And only four years later he was!

At this writing, Steve is the drummer for the Rolling Stones, since Charlie Watts passed away, and one of the most sought-after musical directors in the business. I also wanted to try and bring America into the convention hall. We designed an extremely wide hundred-and-fifty-foot screen, just above the stage. When the convention started, on this long narrow screen we put aerial images—low flying shots of America, waving wheat fields in Kansas, approaching the Statue of Liberty from the Atlantic Ocean, flying above crashing waves on the Pacific Coast approaching the Golden Gate Bridge, and flying over the Gettysburg Memorial. All these shots created the impression that the delegates in Boston understood America and appreciated its unmatched scenic beauty. I contacted Willie Nelson to perform "Living in the Promised Land" and visualized his live performance with spectacular scenes of immigrants arriving at Ellis Island to begin a new life in America. It was truly a goosebump moment.

My seat for calling the show was high atop the center camera cluster, I had a view of everything in the room. With me was my entire team, Bob Dickinson our lighting designer, writers who were making last minute changes, Jim Tanker my associate director, my assistant Jason Uhrmacher, and dozens of telephones that flashed red when a call was coming in instead of ringing a bell. In addition, there were dozens of communication intercoms to crew, writers, teleprompters, network producers from NBC, CBS, CNN etc. Each had their own separate channel as well. On one channel I could speak to Glenn Weiss (director of the world feed), special effects crews which were everywhere in the arena including up in the ceiling, and most importantly to my head stage manager, Garry Hood, who was cueing entrances and exits on my command.

Four days before the convention there was a meeting of all the representatives from television networks, newspapers, and photographers to discuss the outline of the four days of convention events. About eighty-five people were present. When the meeting ended a CNN producer approached me requesting permission to put one of my intercom channels (we called them Private Lines or PL's) on the air as transitions were being made. They thought it would be interesting for their viewers to hear some behind the scenes activity as we worked our way through the four-day convention. I agreed, saying that CNN could take a feed from my TV Network PL, which I was using to tell news directors/producers when certain things were about to happen, for example, "Senator John Kerry will be entering from twenty-eight in forty-five seconds."

Prior to the convention, Ricky Kirshner told me that he received a suggestion from the Democratic Party in Massachusetts that we should hire some local vendors. Everyone we had hired was from either New York or Los Angeles. Ricky and I agreed that we could hire a local company to supply the customary balloon drop at the end of the nominee's acceptance speech on Thursday night. That was a decision that we would later regret.

It was downright thrilling for me to be in this pulsating environment. I kind of felt like I was king of the hill on top of my perch in the center of the arena. The 2004 convention marked the first major party presidential nominating convention to be held since the terrorist attacks of September 11th, 2001. On the first night we created a memorial service to honor the victims of the attacks. Haleema Salie, who lost her daughter, son-in-law, and unborn grandchild, spoke about her pain when American Airlines Flight 11 hit the North Tower of the World Trade Center.

One highlight of the convention was a keynote speech from a young Democratic Senator from Illinois, Barack Obama, that spellbound the crowd. Only four years later Barack Obama would become the President of the United States. He talked about his hope for America, including, "The hope of a skinny boy with a funny name who believes that America has a place for him too."

On Thursday July 29th, 2004, John Kerry was nominated for president by the National Democratic Convention. As he approached the podium he saluted, and his first words were, "I'm John Kerry and I am reporting for duty." Thus began an evening that I've never been able to forget no matter how much I've tried.

When Senator Kerry finished his acceptance speech, I cued the traditional balloon drop. We had one hundred thousand red, white, and blue balloons in drop bags up in the ceiling. "Go balloons!" I shouted on my tech PL intercom. Nothing happened. "Balloons! GO! ... GO! ... GO!" Still nothing. I looked up, and the balloons were still in their drop bags in the ceiling—stuck! Immovable! I panicked. I shouted into my Tech PL to my stage crew "Where are the fucking balloons?" "Where are they, god dammit?" I was really pissed.

Suddenly, my head stage manager, Garry Hood, yelled over my PL, "Don, get off your PL ... now!" What I did not know was that CNN— had accidentally—tapped into my tech PL instead of the network PL and heard me screaming and cursing about the balloons. Stagehands were still tugging at the balloon bags in the ceiling when I realized that everything I had said had been carried live to the world.

Within seconds, dozens of phones on my perch above the convention floor started lighting up. My assistant, Jason Uhrmacher, said, "I don't know what's going on, but all the morning news shows want you to come in tomorrow morning." I was confused and probably in denial when Jason handed me a phone. It was a reporter I knew from USA Today. "Was that you I just heard cursing on CNN? Wolf Blitzer said it was you!" I denied it. I didn't want it to be true, but it was, and I simply lied about it.

I had embarrassed myself in front of the whole world. One thing that bothered me was that this was a result of hiring a local balloon company that said they had experience with massive balloon drops.

What Ricky and I found out later was that their business was primarily creating animal figures with long thin balloons at birthday parties. They loaded the thousands of balloons into their drop bags attached to the ceiling ten days before the convention. Once the convention continued, the heat generated by the lights had raised the temperature of the ceiling significantly, causing the balloons to swell, and by the time we got to the Thursday night balloon drop they were packed into the ceiling grid like sardines ... hot sardines.

As I walked back to my hotel that night, I thought my career was over. When I called my wife, Suzan, she said, "Honey, you overreact to everything." But it sure did hurt.

I was supposed to leave on Friday afternoon but I snuck out of my hotel just as the sun was coming up in Boston, grabbed a cab to the airport, and got the first flight from Boston's Logan airport back to Los Angeles. It was not a pleasant trip home. I must have had three or four Bloody Mary's. I finally drifted asleep, humming one of my favorite songs—Willie Nelson's "Bloody Mary Morning." I was so depressed that I didn't care if the plane crashed, at least that would have taken me out of my misery, but then I shook it off by thinking about my four children at home, I missed them.

Two days later I was driving my kids to school when Jay Leno pulled up beside me on Mulholland Drive and motioned for me to roll down my window. With a big smile he gave me a thumbs-up and yelled, "I didn't know you had it in you, man." I knew then that time would heal the whole thing.

WHEN THE COMMUNIST PARTY PANICKED
SHANGHAI HOSTS THE SPECIAL OLYMPICS

Y ou don't go into producing television and live world events to cause
an international political embarrassment or cause a possible rift between countries, but that is what nearly happened when we agreed to produce the Opening Ceremonies of the Special Olympics World Summer
Games in Shanghai for Chinese Communist leadership in 2007. The fact
that it didn't happen is a testimony to what is possible in this world.

Our company had produced the Opening and Closing Ceremonies
for the Olympic Summer Games in Atlanta in 1996 and the Winter
Games in Salt Lake in 2002, so we weren't that surprised when in 2004,
a delegation from Beijing came to West Hollywood to visit my office
on Beverly Boulevard. Leading the delegation was Dr. Shi De Wong, a
high-profile Chinese executive and president of the Special Olympics
in China, Mary Gu, who had the number two job, and Peter Wheeler
from the Special Olympic Headquarters in Washington. Clearly this
was of great importance to them and the Chinese government; otherwise they would not have made the long trip.

The Special Olympics, founded by Eunice Kennedy Shriver, is
the world's largest sports organization for children and adults with
intellectual and physical disabilities. It provides year-round training
and activities to more than five million athletes in one hundred and
seventy-two countries and allows them to compete in games modeled
after the Olympics.

In our first meeting in Hollywood, which included David Goldberg and Geoff Bennett as producers and Juliane Hare as associate producer, Dr. Shi stressed China's commitment to the Special Olympics and hosting their world summer games in Shanghai three years later on October 7th, 2007. We, of course, knew that a year after that, Beijing would host the regular Summer Olympic Games in 2008. Clearly there was connection, if unspoken.

The Chinese had never hosted such high profile, worldwide event. The Special Olympics Opening Ceremonies would be their first introduction of China to the entire world as well as proof of their ability to deliver a large-scale production equal to the highest world standards, technically and creatively. It would also set the stage for the much larger ceremonies they would produce the next year for the Summer Olympic Games.

In many ways, they saw the Special Olympics as a test they needed to pass with flying colors. It was a matter of the utmost importance at the highest levels.

My company and I had been approached numerous times about producing ceremonies for the Special Olympics, but to be honest, the budgets were so low they hardly covered the cost of lighting the field, let alone a topflight production even on a simpler scale. But money wasn't the problem here. The Chinese were committed to whatever it took to create the highest quality event possible. It was impossible not to be impressed with the seriousness of their intentions and pledge to back up their high aspirations.

There was something else that appealed to me on another level. A true East-West coproduction would give us the chance to work with the best Chinese artists—scenic designers, costume designers, musicians, composers, and choreographers. Chinese culture is rich in symbolism and mythology from its 6000-year-old history. It is a country full of sensibilities and traditions that are different than ours. There was a lot to learn and a lot to share. There was also a surprise bonus, in the form of a thousand soldiers from the People's Republic of China's Red Army, who were put at our disposal to use as stagehands, drummers, dancers, or anything we wanted them to be. This eliminated one of the biggest headaches of large-scale productions. Manpower.

We would provide the overall creative leadership and management of the ceremonies as well as lighting design and sound engineers. We would invite Western artists such as Yo-Yo Ma, Tan Dun, Jackie Chan, and Quincy Jones who had performed previously with Chinese artists to join us.

I soon developed the greatest respect for our Chinese partners and their remarkable cultural history. Yes, there were hurdles that complicated everything, starting with the simple act of translation, which turned out to be not simple at all.

The first day, it was ridiculously time consuming, as each side had to wait for the translation to respond. After that, we switched to the UN system—translators in soundproof booths simultaneously translating Mandarin and English into the headsets we all would wear. It certainly sped thing up, and fact-based information translated easily, but subjective concepts—how we wanted viewers to feel or emotions we hoped would be reflected in the choreography and costumes and music— were much harder to communicate in one language, let along two.

Each day was filled with surprises I had never experienced in decades of working in my job. One example occurred early one morning when I arrived at the stadium and saw a group of about ten Chinese officials walking through the stadium seats checking sound levels. When I inquired what they were doing, they said, "We are checking sound levels because President Hu Jintao will be declaring the games officially open, and when President Hu speaks, his sound must be three times louder than any other sound heard in the ceremonies."

Another example involved the Public Safety Bureau Officer (PSB). Every public event in China is assigned one, and he's at your side anytime anything is going on the field—from load in, construction, and rehearsals, to the show itself and later even the strike out. Eleven days before the show, we were rehearsing fifteen hundred dancers who were creating an ocean on the floor of the field with waving blue silk fabric. A Chinese junk would later "sail" through the ocean and exit on the opposite side of the field. It was very hot that day in August, and when I decided to give the dancers a break, they laid down on the field to rest. Unexpectedly, the junk appeared and started moving across the field at full speed directly toward the dancers scattered all around, threatening to run them over. I instantly yelled into the stadium speakers, "STAP!" (Mandarin for stop).

The PSB Officer was standing behind me and said to me in broken English, "Mr. Mischer, unlike your country, I just want you to know that if the junk would have run over and killed a dancer, the limit of your liability would have been only $20,000 dollars ... and it often happens here in China, especially in construction."

During this whole process, I learned there could be benefits to living under a dictatorship such as the Communist Party in China. If a road was to be built through a residential neighborhood, or a block leveled to create a park, there were no meetings and community hearings to discuss it. It just happened.

About six weeks before the Opening Ceremonies, we had to fly from Shanghai, where we worked, to Beijing to present our creative plan to the highest-ranking Communist Party members, a meeting of supreme importance. Our team boarded a China Eastern Airlines flight in plenty of time to make the 7:00 PM meeting in Beijing. Traveling with us was the third ranking Communist in the country, Deputy Party Secretary of Shanghai, Madame Ying. However, violent thunderstorms around the airport kept delaying all flights, and we waited on the tarmac as the storms continued. The captain spoke over the loudspeaker, first in Mandarin and then in English, "Ladies and Gentlemen. We are number twenty-six in line for take-off and could be waiting here for possibly two hours. So, we're going to serve you lunch while we sit on the tarmac."

Lunch was served, but before we finished eating, the flight crew suddenly scurried through the cabin collecting our trays. The weather was improving, and a clearly surprised pilot got back on the intercom and said, "We've just gotten permission to take off first. Please fasten your seat belts immediately." I couldn't believe it.

I looked out my window and saw our plane pull out of line and pass ahead of twenty-five airplanes waiting to take off. Why? It seems the party leaders in Beijing did not want to be kept waiting. They knew Madame Ying was on our flight and got ahold of Shanghai's flight control to tell them that China Eastern Airlines Flight 89 must take off first. We walked into our meeting five minutes early!

The meeting went very well. The Chinese authorities were happy with our concept, our bookings, our scenery, music, and costumes, and we returned to Shanghai feeling very good about where we were. But that feeling did not last long.

The night of our first rehearsal was ten days before the Opening Ceremonies. It wasn't a rehearsal, it was what we call a "put together," the first time that all the show's segments are rehearsed in show order. These "put-togethers" are always train wrecks; jerky starts and stops, casts coming from the wrong places, people getting confused and sometimes even bumping into each other during their exits and entrances, lighting is terrible, graphics and film inserts aren't finished yet. "Put togethers" are terrible for anybody who is watching, including me and our creative team as we see all our wonderful creative ideas completely fall apart. It's also when we clearly see what needs to be fixed to connect things smoothly. I should mention however, that the People's Liberation Army was perfect. These soldiers did not make mistakes. They nailed it. I remember thinking, "I hope we never have to fight these guys in a war because they are clearly very, very disciplined, and awfully strong."

Like all "put togethers" this one was closed to the public. No press or cameras, no families or girlfriends and boyfriends of cast members were allowed in the stadium. I continued to stress the element of surprise as I do in all my productions. I didn't want to take any chances with seeing what we were doing written all over the next day's newspapers.

I learned that lesson the hard way, at the 1996 Atlanta Olympics. The city's newspaper, the *Atlanta Journal Constitution*, had sneaked a camera and a journalist to the top of an arena roof one block away from the stadium, to photograph the entire Opening Ceremonies dress rehearsal. The morning before the show, a special edition of the paper laid out everything, which took the wind out of my sails, spoiling what should have been the wonderful surprises in store for the audience, that we had all been working on for more than three years. Thankfully in Shanghai, I had managed to keep most things a secret.

However, there were other elements I had never encountered in all my years of dealing with Olympic host cities, international protocol committees, network higher ups, and Hollywood studio heads and agents. Unbeknownst to us, eight uninvited, top-ranking members of the Communist Party slipped into the stadium to watch that rehearsal from high up seats. Had I known about it, I would have never started until I got them out.

What they saw at the first "put together" scared them, of course. It scared me too. That night, about 1:00 AM, I received a message that there would be an emergency meeting in the morning with the party leaders, our staff and CCTV (China Central Television), the Chinese government's television networks.

I barely slept. I sensed trouble ahead, that there would be a lot of frightened and angry party members complaining about all the things that went wrong. When I walked into the meeting, there were eighty people waiting for me.

They had all come to declare that the Opening ceremonies for the Special Olympics should be taken away from Don Mischer Productions and given to CCTV, as the party trusted them to do a better job. A barrage of heated, loud voices hurled across the room.

Honestly, my concern was not so much about a power struggle or a matter of pride, but rather helping them realize that if we turned over a massive twenty-seven-million-dollar show with thousands of cast members, and hundreds of lighting, music, and special effects cues, just a few days before the actual show, it would be an unmitigated disaster. CCTV was an impressive operation. I had a good relationship with their director, Zhang Xiaohai, but he was completely unfamiliar with all the thousands of elements in the show. We had spent three years creating, designing, building sets, rehearsing the cast, and managing everything, and I knew every inch of all of them. I also knew, from experience that it takes about two or three more rehearsals to smooth things out and begin to gain some confidence.

Accusations flared up like a wildfire, and while I may have not expressed myself as calmly as I could have, I remained firm that they would make an irreparable mistake to switch producers now. The show would fall on its face, and all of us—China, the Communist Party, the city of Shanghai, CCTV, our truly wonderful East/West co-production team, would be blamed.

I felt especially bad for the Chinese Special Olympics team, Dr. Shi, Mary Gu, Polly Wong, and Madame Ying in the Shanghai city administration, who would catch hell and lose face for hiring a Western production company.

At one point I got so frustrated, trying to protect them from having things fall apart, that I threw up my hands and shouted, "Okay, you take over the fucking show, but you have no clue what you're doing!"

There was silence in the room. The red-faced interpreter whispered in my ear, "I can't translate what you just said, because I'll get fired."

Then Bob Dickinson, our lighting designer, slipped me a note that said, "We better order two vans to take us to the American embassy in Shanghai because I'm not sure we're ever going to get out of here." David Goldberg, our co-producer agreed; they were serious.

Dr. Shi, Mary Gu, Polly Wong, and several of our Chinese creative team came to our defense, putting their own jobs on the line to defend us. They supported our ability and experienced know-how, to get quickly from the "put together" to a polished show. We had been working closely together since the beginning, and our trust in one another was mutual. Their willingness to continue supporting us is what allowed us to keep our jobs and for the rehearsals to continue.

The Special Olympics Opening Ceremonies went on without a hitch. In fact, they were declared a smash hit.

Especially praised were the martial artist demonstrations...and the "human tower"—four levels of people standing on each other's shoulders, up which two special athletes climbed. Once they reached the top, beaming with pride, the audience gave them a standing ovation for their spectacular feat. President Hu Jintau was particularly pleased and rose to his feet, clapping with exuberant applause.

Dr. Shi and Mary Gu had helped us bring acclaimed Western artists to the ceremonies. Yo-Yo Ma and Lang Lang performed with the

Shanghai Symphony. The actors Colin Farrell and Jackie Chan presented several acts. Quincy Jones closed the show with a song he wrote to
celebrate the Chinese commitment to Special Olympians. The Opening
Ceremony aired over four separate Chinese television networks all run
by CCTV. It was broadcast in America by ABC and worldwide by the
BBC. The morning after the show, the press in Shanghai and all over
China ran overwhelmingly positive headlines, "WE DID IT!" and "China Opened the Door To the World Last Night!"In China, press con-
ferences and meetings were held for days following the show with curious reporters eager to know how we did it and just to praise the show.
The BBC said of the opening ceremony, "it was visually striking with
dazzling lighting, fireworks, costumes, and overwhelmingly emotional
music." And the *Wall Street Journal* observed, "The opening ceremony
of the 2007 Special Olympics was the first major international broadcast emanating from modern day China. Eighty thousand fans filled
Shanghai stadium as hundreds of millions of viewers around the world
tuned in. The theme, 'Harmony: The Common Dream of Humanity'
captured the country's ancient culture and promoted the spirit of harmony among the 165 nations that participated."

In the United States, President George W. Bush hosted the Torch
Run around the United States at a White House ceremony in the Rose
Garden. The entire torch run was broadcast live in America by the
National Geographic Channel.

The 2007 Special Olympics World Summer Games were considered China's largest global sports and humanitarian effort event in
their history. Later on, books were written to extol how well those
ceremonies were received around the world. Mary Gu was named as
one of the twenty iconic Chinese women by the famous French magazine *ELLE*, for her outstanding achievement in such an influential
organization.

The successful staging of the games had reflected well not just on Mary Gu, who now is president of CAA China, but also on Dr. Shi, the two people who had first walked into my office three years earlier. A genuine warmth had grown between us, and with the entire Chinese team, and we wanted to share the triumph with all of them. So, we decided to host a dinner for everyone at our home in Los Angeles. It was a wonderfully warm evening full of heartfelt remarks, many spoken in Mandarin. Dr. Shi made a gracious toast as everyone raised their glasses. One of my favorite moments was when Yan Wen, our Chinese scenic designer, nicknamed Moto, introduced his wife whom he called Rola, a twosome we later nicknamed "Motorola." Our son, Charlie, and young daughter, Lilly, sat off to the side, amazed by the languages and how we all communicated, with and without translations. One word they understood clearly was my name, and laughingly told me later how strange it seemed to hear people talking rapidly in Mandarin, then hear the name, "Don Mischer," pop up in the middle of an otherwise unintelligible sentence.

We have remained good friends with our Chinese partners and stay in regular contact, talking about what's happening in our own lives and around the world. We share the unique experience of having worked together on the first co-production between two completely different cultures on a major international event.

It left me with a profound understanding about something I hadn't really thought about before. When countries are in conflict, rattling their sabers at one another until nearly a breaking point, people can still come together on a personal level, developing bonds of friendship and trust that let them break through the impasse and dispel the anger, something big governments can't do. It changes everything, to work with one another as fellow human beings, not enemies, finding solutions together as you go.

This world would be a different place if there were more face-to-face personal connections, working relationships such as we had on our massive event, when everyone shared the same hopes, dreams, and concerns. Despite all the things we didn't have in common, we faced the impasses and ideas together, wrestled with problems and decisions as one team, standing on each other's shoulder just as those special Olympic athletes had.

It made the Opening Ceremonies not only possible, but a triumph. That's what I took from the Shanghai World Summer Special Olympics Opening Ceremonies. And I don't think it gets much better than that.

THE OPENING CEREMONIES OF THE SALT LAKE WINTER OLYMPICS
FRAGILE BUT TOGETHER AFTER 9/11

The things that keep me up at night rarely turn out to be the biggest problems. It is the unexpected that always gets you, something so far out of your thinking you are stunned in near disbelief, which is what happened when we produced the Opening Ceremonies for the Winter Olympics in Salt Lake City in 2002. You have to be ready to think at full speed, lead with your best instincts, trust your heart and your team.

The Salt Lake Games were run by Mitt Romney who had come in at the urgent request of the Mormon Church to clean out the scandals plaguing the Games and the International Committee over bribery and influence peddling, which had begun to sour the influence of the original Olympic ideals. Romney was an honest broker, a highly successful businessman and Mormon who possessed a sense of clarity, managerial talents, and vision for the future of Olympic Games. He made strong, unexpected choices, one of which was choosing my company over fifty-two larger, much fancier organizations to produce the Opening and Closing Ceremonies.

Romney, who was a big thinker, described our offices on Beverly Boulevard in Los Angeles as tiny and slightly underwhelming, compared to the imposing size and flashiness of companies like Universal Television and the Walt Disney Company who also bid on the Ceremonies.

We were a mid-sized company, without a press wing or waiting room of expensive furniture. Romney liked our previous work, including the Opening Ceremonies for the Atlanta Summer Games, but what sold him on us was that we emphasized looking for emotional connections with the audience, which was in keeping with his mission to restore the original spirit of the Olympics. I am never comfortable hyping things up or overselling a pitch for a job, but rather (and prefer) to point out the challenges, which turned out to be right up Romney's alley. He appreciated my straightforward understatement and admissions of past missteps.

The Ceremonies, an enormous undertaking made of emotions, spectacle, and symbolic traditions, are a feather in the cap of any producer, but before I accepted the job, I had to get Romney's word that I would report to him directly, rather than to intermediaries who translate and often miscommunicate your ideas. It can turn the fast-paced pressure of creative decisions, for which I am responsible, into a bureaucratic quagmire. As it turned out, rapidly changing events made time and trust of the essence.

I had spent a year putting our pitch together with choreographer Kenny Ortega, costume and set designer Peter Minshall, and my ace co-producers, David Goldberg and Geoff Bennett, the people whose imaginations and know how laid out our blueprint. We were a close-knit group, and having produced the Atlanta Olympic Ceremonies together, knew what lay ahead of us—three years of crammed intensity.

We enlisted hundreds of craftsmen and technicians in music, costume, dance, lighting, and stagecraft. We contacted artists to perform, commissioned music, secured thousands of volunteers and extras who we could not pay. We brought in truckloads of equipment, met with firework experts, and set out contingency plans for every problem we'd ever encountered or heard about.

We studied the history of Utah, because Opening Ceremonies serve both to welcome the world to the Olympic games and give a warm introduction of the host city. We would tell a little of Utah's rise out of the Old West, as settlers came in covered wagons and then by railroad to a land of natural beauty and enchantment, as well as a place of mountains and deserts, bears, wild horses, elks, and bison—all of which we created with stadium sized, fantasy like imagery, designed by Michael Curry who designed Broadway's *Lion King*.

The many tribes of Native Americans are integral to Utah's story, and I got to visit far off areas to meet with leaders and tribal councils. Each nation requested they enter and be recognized on its own. However, it was my strong belief that a way had to be found to convince them to also join together by the end, despite being warned this would never happen. It was so essential for these Games to reflect and reinforce the original spirit of the Olympics, that I didn't care how long or how many trips to the remote reservations it took to get us there. In the end, one of the most moving elements in the Ceremonies was a full out dancing by five Native American Nations to one unified drumbeat.

A thousand ideas are traded back and forth, and I find that the good ones rise to the top. Then, after about three meetings, the best of those are the ones I'm still thinking about. The logistics to turn these ideas into reality take volumes of detailed notebooks. Spectacle takes a lot of a care. There's a cast of 8,500 people, ranging from age eight to tribal elders, who have to be rehearsed and fed, huge fields of loading areas prepared, lighting tested, electrical work installed, firework displays mounted, the massive ice floor for the center created and the seventy-two foot glass and steel Olympic cauldron built.

We commissioned two original musical scores. Michael Kamen and Brian May wrote the theme, "Light the Fire Within," to underscore the first portion of the ceremonies—a ten-minute drama on ice that told the story of a child of light. A young boy, lantern in hand, would skate across the stadium's ice rink floor, battling storms, so he could share his light with other children, and ultimately with all 65,000 present in Olympic Stadium. The storms were created by giant turbulent storm clouds designed by Peter Minshall, dramatic music, lighting, and sound effects. For another section of the show, I asked John Williams, who had written for three previous Olympics if he would compose something for us to reflect the Olympics' core beliefs. He suggested a symphonic work for the Utah Symphony that could take advantage of the 360 voices of the famous Mormon Tabernacle Choir. He imagined them singing not lyrics but rather uniting their voices into the sound of one powerful human instrument, invoking the motto of the Olympics, in a stirring piece called "Call of the Champions."

It's meetings like these, as I listened to creative minds turn abstract ideas from mere slogans into tangible works with emotional reach, that make my sleepless nights and nail-biting afternoons melt away. It lifts you into another level and makes my job and my life rich beyond compare. I'd walk away from meetings like a grown-up-producer but inside I felt like a kid skipping down the street.

Things began to fall into place. I could feel the excitement mount as sketches took concrete shape, fireworks and choruses successfully rehearsed, but of course I still worried all the time. There isn't one moment when I didn't remember something I forgot to worry about. With only five months left, there was still much to do.

And then it happened. What could never even have been imagined. The entire world went dark. Terrorists had hijacked four planes and struck them into the heart of America. On September 11th, two planes hit the World Trade Center, one the Pentagon, and one crashed in Pennsylvania before it could hit the nation's capital. Thousands died, and flames engulfed the skies. The entire world was in shock.

There was no clear idea of what would happen next. Things seemed to come to a standstill, as events everywhere were canceled. Life felt suspended. Would the Winter Olympics still go on? They carried years of hopes and planning. We had to assume they would, at the same time it was clear that the Salt Lake Olympic Opening Ceremonies would be the first time all the countries of the world would come together in peace, and on American soil, a country with a broken heart.

We looked at one another, as our own disbelief and tears gave way, to face the pressing questions of how we address all that had happened with both strength and delicacy. Public events carry enormous symbolic weight. Every small thing conveys a clear message, and in an event that is carried live to millions of people speaking different languages, every image says so much, and must be calibrated with care.

This international Olympic gathering had taken on an unforeseen meaning. The Opening Ceremonies in an American city carried a heightened symbolic importance. We felt that the Olympic themes— hopes for unity and peace—were well covered in the two-hour artistic portions of the Opening Ceremonies.

All my instincts told me that the emotional weight of the moment would be felt most during the portions with the Olympic protocols, the established rituals that brought out the athletes and the enduring symbols of the Games. Rituals carry great symbolic and ceremonial weight and can speak most directly to people's worried hearts.

I felt strongly that these moments should convey signs of the world being united, to offer a sense of an on-going security in our lives, and avoid the heat of anger, rancor, or bombast. Somewhat frantically, but very carefully we looked for places in the closing protocols where we could do that.

That portion of the Ceremonies which comes near the end of the three-hour ceremonies, begins with the parade of athletes, who enter behind their country's flag, to great cheering in the stands. After that, the Olympic flag is brought into the stadium. Traditionally it is carried by eight past Olympic medalists from the host city, but what if it were carried by eight respected and beloved people from around the world and different walks of life? A symbolic image that would say so much.

After numerous and immediate discussions with Mitt Romney and Scott Givens from the Salt Lake Olympic Committee, the eight people we asked were Archbishop Desmond Tutu, John Glenn, Steven Spielberg, Lech Walesa, Jean-Michel Cousteau and the Olympic champions Jean-Claude Killy, Cathy Freeman, and Kazuyoshi Funaki. They set the tone of the protocols to follow and were greeted with stunned surprise and emotional applause.

After the flag, came the release of symbolic doves, the symbols of peace. Usually, a lot of time is spent coming up with ever more clever ways to wow the crowd, but instead we turned our focus to the music for the section, where the core of emotions lives. I'm not sure how this song came to me, but it leapt out so clearly, like a sign, because wasn't it how we were all feeling. "Fragile," by Sting.

Sting agreed right away to sing it, and I asked the great cellist and humanist Yo-Yo Ma, who I had the good fortune and joy of working with before, if he would accompany Sting. One of the great perks of my job is coming up with unexpected combinations of artists who together take the music to a whole other level. They both leapt at the chance to play a part in this now weighted ceremony, and our job was to find a way for them to perform this lyrical, delicate song to a stadium of 65,000 people.

The center arena was a field of ice, but with fogging machines we could create the look of mist hovering just above it, like a cloud washed in a pale blue light. The first sounds you heard were Yo-Yo's long, deep notes on the cello, as he and Sting, seated on a disc twenty feet wide and six inches off the ground, slowly floated through the mist towards the center of the ice.

As Sting began to sing, how fragile we are, how fragile we are, the whole stadium seemed to breathe in unison with the notes and the mood, as if saying yes to the sentiments. As Sting neared the end of the song, thirty-six skaters came out from different entrances, carrying dove shaped kites on tall sticks. They skated around Sting and Yo-Yo like angels on ice, until the very last note when they skated out of sight, as if releasing the doves. The lights faded out on Sting and Yo-Yo, as the memory, fragile and kind, hovered in the air. It was a haunting moment.

The last protocol is the most famous moment in the Olympics ceremony, the lighting of the Olympic cauldron. Most of this had been decided before 9/11 but it turned into the most fitting and moving ending possible. After the torch entered the stadium, the last two athletes to hold it passed it to Mike Eruzione, the captain of the US Olympic ice hockey team, whose win over the Russian team in 1980 was called the "Miracle on Ice." He was joined by his teammates to light the cauldron together. There they stood, brimming with joy, their legendary win against the odds had emerged from their trust and strength in one another, and seemed to say everything.

What we did change was that instead of the usual giant scenic spectacle as a finale, we ended the ceremonies by going back to the simplest way to say something else clearly. We did it with one skater, kerosene and the ice itself. One skater sped over the ice, sparks flying off his skates, and he skated around what looked like a giant empty sheet of ice. But as the skater sped over the ice and the invisible kerosene, rings of dazzling fire began to take shape—creating Olympic rings of fire burning on ice. Simple but eloquent. The glow of the Olympics' interlocking rings—fire and ice—ended the evening.

With everything that had been poured into every minute of the ceremonies, the most powerful moment came not at the end, but in the opening moments. Never had a beginning been so crucial or done so much in so few and nearly wordless minutes.

It is customary, after a brief countdown and short artistic introduction, to start the ceremonies with the host country singing its National Anthem while raising its flag. But this was no ordinary moment, because it had only been five months since 9/11, and America still had a gaping hole in her heart. We knew we couldn't just sing the anthem as if nothing had happened.

I had several intense conversations with Mitt Romney and Scott Givens. We agreed we had to keep to protocol while living up to the emotional gravity of the moment. I don't remember which one of us said it first, but the moment someone said it, we all knew what had to be done, and got in touch with officials in New York right away.

At the same time, we still had to the jump through hoops with the IOC officials to carry off my secret plan. Strict rules had been enforced since the Berlin-Nazi Games of 1936 about the use and number of national flags, allowing only one to be shown and only during the national anthem. For my idea to work, we had to get permission to circumvent that, which took more calls that almost anything else.

The moment finally came at the top of the Opening Ceremonies. I cued the announcer to say, as customary first in French and then in English, one simple line, "Ladies and Gentlemen, the American flag that flew at the World Trade Center on September 11th is now being carried into the stadium."

An eerie hush fell over the entire stadium. The crowd of 65,000 people, always an excited and rowdy bunch, dropped their cups and their talking, and stood up without prompting or hesitation. Total strangers

united in a powerful silence. I've never experienced anything like it—
no music, no crowd whispering—just total silence as they watched.

Eight American athletes entered the stadium, with no music or
fanfare—holding the tattered and torn American flag that had been
discovered deep beneath the ruble of the World Trade Center.
An honor guard of New York Police and Firemen walked by their side.

As this solemn procession slowly made its way toward center ice,
we arranged to have Ron de Moraes, director of the world television
feed, cut live to American servicemen 7,215 miles away standing at
attention in Afghanistan.

Tears streamed down the faces of athletes and spectators. From my
show director's perch in a box high above the stadium, I looked around
at all the faces to help find shots Ron could share with the worldwide
television audience.

Then I saw President Bush standing next to Mitt Romney and
Jacques Rogge, president of the International Olympic Committee. Bush stood without moving, his eyes firmly on the flag, as tears
rolled down his checks. It took only a few minutes, and it didn't
politicize the moment in any way, but it touched people far beyond
any words. It said to Americans and the world—we were hurt, we
were torn, but we are here now, together with you. Life will go. Life
will triumph.

The tattered flag finally reached the front of the stage where the
Utah Symphony and ten rows of the Mormon Tabernacle waited. I had to wipe away my own tears, so I could speak clearly into
the headset. "National Anthem...go!" I had asked the choir and
symphony directors to add a slower, more dramatic repeat of the last
four lines of the anthem:

"Oh say does that star-spangled banner yet wave,
O're the land of the free and the home of the brave!"

Over this emotional repeat, a second, new American flag, waving briskly in the breeze, rose to the top of the flagpole, high above the ripped and tattered 9/11 flag being held horizontally by the NYFD and NYPD.

I felt the Olympic Winter Games in Salt Lake City could now truly begin.

THE DAY WE CAME TOGETHER TO REMEMBER THE DAY WE'LL NEVER FORGET
THE CEREMONIES FOR 9/11

This is a televised event I wished had never been necessary to do. The one I felt the most responsibility to get right. It wasn't exactly a television program, but it was carried live by all the television networks and watched by the entire country and many places around the world as well.

The event was the first ceremony held at Ground Zero in New York City, to mark one year since that dark day we call 9/11. The tears of the country weren't yet dry. The families were bereft. This would be the first time the families and the city would come together to mourn and remember.

The person who called me was Patti Harris, Deputy Mayor to the newly elected Mayor of New York City, Michael Bloomberg. It was late February 2002, and I had just finished producing the Closing Ceremonies for the Salt Lake City Winter Olympics. In the Salt Lake Opening Olympic Ceremonies, we had NYPD and NYFD carrying in the tattered flag that once flew atop the World Trade Center north tower, into the stadium. You could have heard a pin drop. It was a powerful moment for me and everyone who witnessed it.

Patti asked me to meet with Mayor Bloomberg in New York to discuss creating this all-important, first commemoration at the site. Apparently, film producer Jeffrey Katzenberg, after talking with Mayor Bloomberg, had told the mayor, "Get someone who knows how to do this right—

talk to Mischer." I felt honored to be asked, and at the same time, fully aware we would be creating not a show but a national ceremony, for which there was no precedent. It had to have both delicacy and depth, emotion and respect, and be carried off without a hitch. It would call on everything I knew as a professional and felt as an American and a human being.

I remember my own horror and stunned disbelief when I saw the events unfold on television. My wife, Suzan, was making breakfast for our nine-year-old son, Charlie, and five-year-old daughter, Lilly, as we gathered around the TV. They were confused and asked me questions for which I had no answer. Why would anyone do that? What happened to all those people in the buildings? Did the hijackers die too? Why? I kept asking myself. How many little nine-year-old boys and five-year-old girls had lost their mother or father that day? What would I say to them? How does one even begin? We understood that whatever we did, would have to work on many levels to give the families of the 2,983 people who died, a way and place to grieve, provide the city ways to come together, and pay tribute to the brave first responders. It would also have to give the country a place to turn, a connection everyone needed.

All of us involved had a hard time agreeing on just how to go about the remembering. At the beginning, I had a somewhat rocky relationship with the mayor who was understandably concerned. He didn't want anything too Hollywood, too "event spectacle." Neither did we, but I also knew it had to have size.

We'd never worked together, and perhaps the mayor didn't yet trust us to handle complicated logistics and the precise timing that so many moving parts required, such as when we brought different elements together at exactly the right moment and in the right place. There was also the question of involving several official branches of police, fire department, and the Port Authority, and various city agencies. Timing was something I knew in my bones. Learning to bring together various agencies was not new to us. Tricky but not new.

Every idea and suggestion was looked over—argued over—by a hundred eyes, including the mayor's. What we did all agree on was that it had to be full of heart, not politics or speeches. And nothing divisive or bombastic. Yet, all there was on the site was this deep hole in the earth, the dust, and debris of destruction.

We came up with a mix of traditional and new rituals, the eloquence of music and the sight of tearstained faces. Sometimes honored words borrowed from American history, and some personal remarks that framed the number of dead in personal terms. And in the end, a symbolic way for the city to lock its arms around the families.

My initial team was small, David Goldberg (co-producer), Sara Lukinson (writer/producer), Maureen Kelly (an all-around girl Friday who could do anything), and Diana Barton (a professor at Emerson College in Boston who compiled the 2,983 names of people who perished on 9/11). We worked in a tiny, cramped office in a downtown city building across the street from City Hall. Sometimes we'd act things out in a corner of the room. We were also getting suggestions from all directions.

Music? Yes, but by who? Moments of silence, yes, but no release of doves or white inflatable spheres for each person who died. Who should be asked to speak? How long should the ceremony last? All morning or an hour? How long does it take to honor the death of 2,983 innocent people by acts of terrorism? Not soldiers, or heads of state, just people like you and me going about our day.

At the first 9/11 Commemoration in 2002, Ground Zero was a huge pit six stories deep, something that felt like an open wound, with only a few heavy metal beams and the tall concrete slurry wall standing as remaining fragments. This was the spot where the families wanted to come—the hole where the North Tower once stood and was the only gravesite they'd ever have. A long ramp was built for excavation from street level down six stories into the pit, which also enabled the families to walk down easily and safely to the bedrock bottom.

I tried to envision what that would look like, after people went down the ramp. I knew we needed a focal point, a place for them to walk to or stand around. A pool of water seemed like the best idea, which would also give them a place to put the flowers and help the flowers stay alive.

I thought it important to begin the entire ceremony by establishing right away that the city was joining together for this, just as they had that day one year ago. We decided on something both symbolic and moving. We asked bagpipers and drummers from the NYPD who traditionally played at the funerals of fallen heroes, to start out from each of the five boroughs. Each group would begin before daybreak, walk through city streets, across the Brooklyn Bridge or on the Staten Island Ferry so they would converge at Ground Zero at exactly the same time. We had spotters along the routes to let us know where each processional was, so we could speed them up or slow them down. They would meet together at the makeshift stage we built on the street level of West Street, adjacent to the pit. Dozens of police would block off West Street and divert traffic.

The bagpiper-led processionals from all five boroughs played until they converged at the West Street stage at 8:44 AM. Mayor Bloomberg then stepped forward to begin the ceremony, asking everyone to join in the first moment of silence at precisely 8:46 AM, marking the time American Airlines Flight 11 hit the North Tower.

There were six life changing moments on 9/11, and we wanted to mark each of them in accordance with when they happened.

The plane hitting the North Tower, then the South Tower, the crash of the plane at Shanksville, the plane hitting the Pentagon and the collapse of Tower One and then Tower Two.

After each of these moments of silence, a uniformed member of the FDNY would ring a small bell on the stage. I thought of that famous line, ask not for whom the bell tolls, it tolls for thee. How we all have a connection to one another, and those who died. We had told the networks the significance of each moment of silence, so they could tell the TV audience.

To this day I still get a pit in my stomach as I count down to the first bell marking the moment the first Tower was hit, and the unfathomable events of the day began.

Mayor Bloomberg was insistent that the ceremony would not be used as a platform for politics or speeches, which allowed us to keep the focus where it should be. Other than Mayor Bloomberg, who spoke poignantly to set up each element of the ceremony, only Governor Pataki of New York and Governor McGreevey of New Jersey would speak. Since Ground Zero was now a part of America's history, Sara Lukinson suggested two passages from our history to reflect that. Governor Pataki read Lincoln's Gettysburg address, which spoke of honoring the dead and hallowing the ground. Governor McGreevey read from the Declaration of Independence, reaffirming America's highest ideals. And to this day, no political speeches have ever been spoken at the annual ceremonies.

One of the biggest points of discussion was how to honor the individuality of the 2,983 victims. Each family would want the name of their loved one said out loud, but the four hours it would take to do that was of some concern. Would families leave after hearing the name they came for, and officials start to go back to work, leaving the last of the families nearly alone?

Not to read all the names would feel as if everyone who died was being lumped into a faceless number. I feel that if you going to do something, you have to carry it out all the way in order to let the emotions play out—to be what they need to be need. Even if that was four hours.

In the end, it was the reading of the list of names that brought a dignity and moving eloquence to the ceremony. The only thing that captured the enormity of the loss and gave each death the honor of a name and being a real person. As much as this was a national ceremony, it was also a personal one for each family. Families did stay, walking down the ramp, holding up their handmade signs, with the faces of their husbands, wives, daughters, sons, siblings, and friends. They wanted to be there as long as they could.

I did feel, however, that it was crucial to have two family members give short personal remarks, to lend a personal framework to all the names spoken. Some thought the families would object to singling out just two people, but it always works the opposite way. Their words echo your own feelings.

How brave it was of the two young daughters, one eleven years old and the other just twenty, to accept our invitation to speak. One recited a simple and loving poem to her father, Benjamin Clark, a chef who worked on the 96th Floor. The other read a tribute to her stepfather, Franco Lalama, a Port Authority engineer who worked on the 64th floor. She ended by saying, "I think he knows how much I loved him. In my eyes he died a hero and how much more could you ask for." The next day, the papers wrote about the moving simplicity of their words which touched the center of everyone's similar feelings.

Music speaks to the heart, and I knew that a gentle musical underscoring, would lend a poignancy to the long reading of the names. The first person I asked was Yo-Yo Ma—a cellist of deep soulfulness, and someone I had had the pleasure of working with before.

He jumped at this chance and chose to play a mournful excerpt from Bach's 5th Cello Suite.

He sat on the side of the small stage where the readers stood and began to play as the reading of the names began. After him, musicians played until the end, including a Juilliard String quartet, flautist Paula Robison, the violinist Gil Shaham, the guitarist Sharon Isbin, and the St. Paul String Quartet.

When you create a live event, you can never predict what unexpected thing might enhance or spoil your best laid plans. That morning, it was nature herself.

After the reading of the names began, and Yo-Yo started to play, a sudden wind came out of nowhere. Fierce and ferocious, it whipped up everything. All the dust from the bottom and sides of the pit circled up like a dust tornado, rising hundreds of feet up into the sky.

Yo-Yo's music stand blew away, but knowing the music by heart, he kept playing, while struggling to keep his bow moving across the strings. The Juilliard quartet started to play but had to stop when their music stands were blown off the stage, and our team scurried to find the stands and music sheets.

It was an accident of nature, but it felt providential. I watched the faces of the families, who seemed stunned, as if this was a message—a sign—that the spirits of their loved ones were there. Ceremonies are remembered for the emotions they express, and that morning, the sudden swirl of wind and dust and memories expressed all the sadness of the day, but also the eternal presence of the people we love, who remain locked in our hearts. When I think about that moment, I still get chills.

The ceremony ended, as ceremonies often do, with "Taps." We placed three trumpeters in different locations around Ground Zero, each starting "Taps" just a split second later, as if it were an echo.

It created a haunting sound that lingered in the air. Four hours after the bagpipers had arrived, the ceremony was over.

The eloquence and power of the ceremony came from the simple reciting of all those names and the sight of the families holding pictures of their loved ones, silently laying roses and carnations at the bottom of the pit, as the names of their loved ones echoed through the wind-swept place where the World Trade Center towers once stood.

It was a day to remember one of the darkest days in our history. At the same time, it was also a day to remember those who had rushed in to help, and those who kept coming, in the days and months to come, to look out for and care for one another.

We continued to produce the ceremony until its twentieth year. The faces and stories of the families and all those we all had come to know at the Memorial, were now part of our lives.

On the tenth anniversary, the transformation of the site into a beautiful memorial park was finally finished. Two black marble inverted fountains had been built on the footprints of the two Towers. Rimming the fountains was a ledge with every name engraved into the marble, allowing flowers, flags, and memorabilia to be placed into the carved names themselves. There were trees and benches. Both President Bush and President Obama took part in the ceremony that year.

We were also there to help create and televise the national dedication by President Obama of the 9/11 Museum. Once again, we featured the faces and stories of those who perished, the first responders and the few who had survived. On the twentieth anniversary all the living presidents attended, watching silently from the side, their bodies ramrod with respect. Bruce Springsteen sang a simple, heartfelt, "I'll See You in My Dreams," as tears trickled down faces of the victims' loved ones. Families read the names and still held up signs, but now they read, "Dad you are a grandfather now, Margaret had two children. You would be so proud."

I ended up growing up with these families. I was witness to the effects of time and healing. I saw how many people had turned their grief into acts of kindness, or grown closer to one another, or found strengths they didn't know they had. And how so many found solace in the annual gathering at this place of final rest.

I never expected that commemorating the events of that tragic day would become part of my life for two decades. An opportunity that came to me because of my previous experiences and wound up becoming an experience which deeply affected me. Each person on our team, the line producer, writer, music organizers, reader coordinators, spotters, and stage mangers—they all asked to return year after year. We all shared the same sense of pride and honor to be there.

THE BOSS
WORKING WITH BRUCE SPRINGSTEEN

There was a running joke in my office that whenever we began a new show, I'd always say Bruce Springsteen would be perfect for this. Everyone would roll their eyes and walk back to their desk, while I called Bruce's guy, Jon Landau, and got the "No, thank you." Then, they would all come back, bringing me a large Frappuccino from Starbucks downstairs and a list of names to call next.

It wasn't just because I had been a longtime fan of Springsteen, it was that whenever a show had something American at its core, like the Closing Ceremonies of the Atlanta or Salt Lake Olympic Games or the Super Bowl halftime I knew how Springsteen stood for something uniquely American to his audience, and could captivate a crowd in both rousing and emotional ways, and even by his presence alone. I always offered him the solo spot, but never got a yes.

I'm not easily discouraged when I produce television shows, because more than half of my time is spent moving on each time I hear, "no, thank you" or "we have a schedule conflict," both of which generally mean "It just doesn't feel right to me." I've always found that if an artist is truly inspired, they will make it happen. Period! For a producer, getting rejected is part of your job description. If you can't handle it, you're in the wrong business. Your skin becomes as thick as a rhino, so you keep going back. But I did feel that doing a show with Springsteen might not be in the cards, even though I'd been shuffling them continuously through the years.

Every director, feature film or television, knows that casting is ninety percent of what makes a scene or song work. Maybe I'd just never found the right part for Springsteen. Or maybe it was never meant to be.

I had worked with Bruce once, when I was co-producing the Kennedy Center Honors in 1997 and he came to pay tribute to Bob Dylan, who would be seated with his fellow Honorees in the box next to President Clinton and First Lady Hillary Clinton. Bruce wanted to sing "The Times They Are A-Changin'" alone, with his acoustic guitar and mouth harmonica, saying a few words beforehand to the audience and Dylan. He had strong feelings about his segment, wanting to create a feeling that was part reverence for the song, and part personal homage to Dylan, and when he came to rehearsals, he was very open to our ideas about how we could achieve that.

I felt that since Springsteen connects so immediately with his audience, and his feeling of respect for Dylan and the song was so strong, we should keep the staging extremely simple and not gussy it up with any special effects. I suggested we have just a single beam of light from above, very simple and very dramatic, so the rest of the stage would fall away into black. Then it would just be him, carrying the entire weight of the segment. He liked the idea and the night of the show, he stood in the pin light, spoke quietly from his heart, and then began to sing, without ever overdoing it. He delivered the moment in way that gave Dylan and his iconic song its due, a timeless work that remains both a reflection and urgent call to our country.

Twelve years passed, with the usual bushel full of "no, thank-yous" from Jon Landau whenever I asked if Bruce would like to do the Super Bowl halftime show.

So I was totally unprepared for a phone call from Jon on Monday morning, February 4th, 2008, the day after Super Bowl XLII. "Hi Don,

Bruce watched the Super Bowl halftime show you did with Tom Petty and would like to do next year's Half time show with you." I answered, as professionally and warmly casual as I could, "Hey Jon, thanks for calling. That's great, we'd love to do that." I hung up the phone and let out a loud and long Whoop. I knew that this was finally going to happen. I felt so euphoric, I told everyone to take the rest of the day off.

We'd already done five halftime shows, with Michael Jackson, Paul McCartney, Prince, the Rolling Stones, and Tom Petty, but for me, this would be a personal favorite. If there is a reward for being willing to hear, "no," all the time, this was it.

A few weeks later, I met with Bruce, Jon Landau, and Charles Coplin at the NFL headquarters on Park Avenue in New York. We began to talk over the show, its song list, how many in the band, the size of the stage, and a list of questions we'd have to tackle as we went along. However, while all that was getting underway, the country was about to undergo a huge sea change. Barack Obama had won the presidential election, and we were asked in late December, with six weeks' notice, to co-produce and direct a huge concert at the Lincoln Memorial on the Sunday afternoon before President-elect Barack Obama's swearing-in. This time when I called Jon Landau, his immediate answer was, "Yes. We would like to be a part of that!"

Suddenly, we were about to do two shows with Springsteen, within weeks of one another. Two entirely different kinds of shows and experiences. One was a spectacle of size and the other a spectacle of hope. One had months to prepare, while the Lincoln Memorial concert was coming up fast, on January 9th, 2009. The Super Bowl preparations would have to wait.

The Lincoln Memorial concert, "We Are One," was a once-in-a-lifetime concert and will get its own chapter in this book. But there was one rehearsal with Bruce that bears special mention here, because it was one of those creative moments in my career that stand out as the real reward for me. It took place in a cold and flimsy tent, the night before the concert.

We had asked Springsteen to open the "We Are One" concert. Jon Landau asked me to suggest what I thought he should sing, and the first thing that came to my mind was Bruce's "The Rising." It seemed so perfectly right for the occasion, this sense of something new and momentous that was rising in the country. Jon loved the idea, and so did Bruce.

For me, nothing elevates a musical moment to its highest power more than a great choir. I am sucker for that sound, and when I suggested it to Bruce, he loved it immediately, as I suspected he would. He understood right away that the lift of their 200 voices and young faces behind him would kick off the program with a resounding, contagious, and celebratory optimism.

We had very little time and few places to rehearse all the acts in the concert, so Bruce and the choir had to meet up the night before the show in a makeshift tent of aluminum scaffolding with canvas stretched over it. It was an especially cold week and by nighttime, it was freezing. The kids from Washington's Eastern High School Choir showed up in big coats and gloves, excited to meet Bruce, but so cold, they hoped the rehearsal wouldn't last too long. I'd worked with this choir many times on the Kennedy Center Honors and knew that under the direction of the great Joyce Garrett, they made a mighty sound, and I hoped Bruce would feel the same way.

I had brought the song and singer and choir together, and now it would be up to them. Bruce welcomed the kids with a huge smile and spoke to them like professional equals. As they gathered around him, he explained how he wanted certain things phrased or words emphasized, when to join him, or go out on their own. He was patient but direct and inspired them in ways that made the kids realize that something special was happening. As they poured their hearts and souls into the song, everyone forgot how cold they were, and the unity between soloist and choir became palpable. "The Rising" took on size and emotion. It took on life.

As I watched, I took a deep breath. This is going to be fantastic. Being in the room when it happens, as ideas come to fruition and take flight, is the real payoff for me. That moment when you sense something new is being born that will connect, galvanize, and inspire the audience. Which was exactly what was happening in that tent.

However great it is to win golden statues and flattering notices in the press, and to be honest, they are pretty nice, what truly makes every sleepless night, moment of doubt, nail-biting anxiety, and thousands of no's worth it, is to be there when the artistic sparks start to fly, and something magical takes shape.

Out of all your ideas—dumb and smart, your penciled scribbles and heated arguments, your guesses, instincts, and experience, you and your team have been part of the process that gave a song, or a staged moment the greatest meaning and emotion it could have. When Bruce and the Eastern High School Choir took the stage to begin the "We Are One" concert, they burst the morning open into a joyous and rousing celebration. There could have been no better way to start the concert that marked the election of the young, vibrant, first African American president of our country.

A few days after that concert, we were back to planning an entirely different kind of concert for Bruce's Super Bowl halftime show. A twelve-minute high-velocity marathon that thrives on energy, electricity, and spectacle to fill a huge and frenzied stadium. It's an immense undertaking, because the halftime show had grown to be the largest annual television event of the year, and the one where the performer has to not only live up to his legend but create a new one that will top the show from the year before.

We'd done five Super Bowls before this, as well as large stadium shows for the Olympics, and were completely familiar with the use of pyrotechnics and fireworks, but I assumed Springsteen, who'd never used things like lasers, fancy lighting, elaborate staging with hundreds of volunteers, fireworks, and pyrotechnics, wouldn't be interested in it. So I never brought it up in our early meetings.

After one of our next meetings, Bruce was on his way out when he leaned back into the room and point blank said to me, "What about the pyro?" To be honest, I was a bit dumbfounded. I had never expected to hear those words coming out of Bruce's mouth. Then I realized that Springsteen understood the dynamics of the half time show as perfectly as he understood the emotional waves that permeated the Lincoln Memorial concert or the homage to Bob Dylan. That this high intensity production and the halftime show is a massive production number as much as or more than it is a concert that requires size and flash. Bruce was absolutely intrigued by it all, like a boy with a new toy, production toys he'd never played with before. He was excited to see everything that we could come up with.

About three weeks before his show on February 1st, 2009, Jon Landau and I sat in in my production trailer in Tampa going through the script and marking every single pyro cue we thought would work with the song list. Pyro in a stadium reverberates like thunder in your chest, and in the right places it accents the music and electrifies the emotion of the song. For the songs Bruce picked, there was plenty we could do. He loved all our ideas, and we went full steam ahead.

In addition, I'm as proud as a new father to say that Bruce asked the Eastern High School Choir who sang with him at the Lincoln Memorial, to join him on his new song in the Super Bowl halftime set, "Working on a Dream" We brought them down to Tampa Bay, a great trip for them in the middle of winter. For the show, when they entered to join him for the song, we bathed the stage and stadium floor in a deep blue light, while 85,000 fans held up pocket-sized flashlights we had given them. It looked like stars moving in the wide heavens. Jon Landau was standing behind me in the truck and said, "This is breathtaking." And it was.

The halftime show was electric. Bruce was an unstoppable energetic force that swept up his audience like a tidal wave, without ever losing his connection to them emotionally. He wanted to say a few words directed to the audience at home, like, put down your guacamole and watch our show. I didn't love the idea but I agreed if he'd let me bring a camera right up to him, so he looked directly into it, which meant looking directly at the folks at home.

While he was singing "Tenth Avenue Freeze-Out," he did a running slide on his knees directly toward a camera which I had placed on the edge of stage right. He was going faster than he expected and slid right off the stage. He hit the cameraman and knocked him off the stage to the turf, all caught live. This became a viral moment which you can still find easily on the internet. Surely this was the greatest shot that this lucky cameraman ever got. And I would love to hear him tell the tale. Bruce ended the show in a blaze of "Glory Days," bathed in a wash of red lights, as the pyro and fireworks shot off into the night sky to bring the finale to its big, wow finish. I think Bruce, unused to all the flash and smoke punctuating his set, loved how it worked together with him and the E Street Band, and everyone wound up having a great time. The ratings went through the roof.

I figured we had our great run with Bruce and never expected there would be one more show in our path together, twelve years later. A turn back to the quiet, for the twentieth anniversary ceremonies that marked the events of 9/11. We had been producing those ceremonies at Ground Zero since the first ones in 2002. We knew everyone at the 9/11 Memorial, and at Mike Bloomberg's office who were still much involved with the Memorial and these ceremonies, and who had first asked us to produce the ceremonies.

For this twentieth anniversary, we expected a large number of families to attend, as well as President Biden, former Presidents Obama and George W. Bush and political dignitaries including past and present senators and governors from New York and New Jersey. They would all be standing to the side, as they did every year, as the names were read, and a few songs were sung. I took a chance and asked if Bruce would sing one song by himself, feeling that on top of this being a national event, many who died were from his home state of New Jersey. He agreed in principal but worried that the press attention he always got would divert attention from the solemnity of the morning, and the remembrance of those who had died. If we guaranteed the secrecy of his appearance, he'd come. If word leaked out, he felt it best to bow out.

For the twenty years we'd done the ceremonies, the Memorial team insisted on knowing everything and everyone who would be involved, seeing them as a reflection of the 9/11 Memorial and families. We'd never lie to them, our trust depended on that, so while rumors flew, we said nothing. Only I and my co-producer David Goldberg knew.

A young advance man for President Biden came to Ground Zero early that morning to ensure all the security precautions were in place and report back to the president's team what was in the ceremony. He wanted to know, said he needed to know, if Bruce Springsteen was going to perform. I said, "I can't confirm that."

Irritated by my answer, he said, "I'm representing the President of the United States, and the President wants to know if Bruce Springsteen is attending!"

I looked him in the eye and said, "I can't tell you." I learned later that he then called Springsteen's office to demand an answer. Jon Landau told me that he never took the phone call when the White House was on the line. Bruce of course, couldn't come to rehearsals, but they sent someone to talk over the staging with me, someone no one knew Bruce was associated with.

That morning, about halfway through the reading of the names, Bruce came out with his acoustic guitar, and sang the most moving version of a song he'd written the year before, "I'll See You in My Dreams." It was about how those we loved and lost still appear to us in our dreams. Even though "our hearts have been emptied," they will always live inside us.

It was a very quiet moment, heartfelt and tender, and said everything that needed to be said that morning. Afterwards, Bruce quietly left the stage and Ground Zero without stopping to speak to anyone. Later I called to thank him, and he said, "I had no idea how emotional it would be hearing all those names read aloud. Thank you for asking me. It was an honor to be there."

A few years later, I saw Bruce's one-man show on Broadway and went backstage to say hello and congratulate him on the truly moving evening. I asked him how it felt to do the same show over and over, week after week. He said he loved it, and the intimacy of the small theater. He greeted me warmly, as if we'd been friends for a long time, and I guess that we had shared enough stages and historical times together to feel that in a way, we were.

TAKING THE STAGE
TOM HANKS AND THE TUSKEGEE AIRMEN

Quincy Jones called me one afternoon in April 2016, which wasn't that unusual, since we'd done several shows together and stayed in touch. This time, he was as excited as I've ever heard him— "Hey man, you've got to do this fantastic gig with me."

He was on the board of the National Museum of African American History and Culture in Washington and had told them they had to "get Mischer on board for the opening weekend." Would I co-produce a two-hour network special with Quincy to celebrate the opening of this new Smithsonian Museum on the National Mall just across the street from the Washington Monument.

My "yes" couldn't come out fast enough. This is the kind of show you dream about. The chance to showcase some of the richest and most influential forms of entertainment in America and take the evening to a whole other level. A way to bring history alive, celebrate an incredibly rich heritage, and play a small part in a long awaited and momentous occasion. The weekend had multiple events at the Museum itself, the Kennedy Center, and the National Mall in Washington. Lou Horvitz would direct the Kennedy Center show and Jonathan X would direct the live dedication the next day on the Mall.

I'd done several specials at American landmarks, such as the reopening of Ellis Island and the 100th anniversary of Carnegie Hall and knew the special thrill that comes with being part of that. How it asks you to rise to the occasion, finding ways to combine exciting performances by top artists with history, stories, and memories that add depth and emotional impact. Where does one even begin?

The Museum was designed with ten levels—five underground and five above—chronologically beginning at the bottom level with artifacts from the earliest days of slavery then moving up through time until finally breaking through into sunlight when you get to the 60s; a decade of significance in the civil rights movement.

Everyone on our team would have to be not only good at what they did, as always, but listen, learn, and dig deep into everything the Museum was about. It had collected the largest treasure trove of African American artifacts, photographs, letters, recordings, tapes, and items—going from slave shackles to Nat Turner's Bible, secret diaries, original manuscripts, photos from civil Rights marches, clips and mementos of top Black athletes, statesmen and entertainers in rock n roll, the blues, Motown, and hip hop. The artifacts overflowed the Museum's ten floors, walls, and even ceilings.

The key to the show would be finding the right balance between the celebratory and the historic, connecting live performances to something held in the Museum. A song or dance, a poem or even a comedy sketch, will always have a stronger impact if we can get the audience to feel the living breath of emotion behind it, the life that those things were was born out of. Not just in political terms, but in personal ways.

We toured the Museum, which was still uncrating boxes, with our eyes and hearts looking hard at everything. Our guide was the tireless and knowledgeable Lonnie Bunch, the Museum's founding director and the guiding force. He asked us to remember that this was a museum of American stories, and that of history of Black and white Americans are linked. Something we felt strongly as we began to approach performers to come to the show.

The Museum covered 400 years of history, and some items began to suggest performance ideas, while others needed further exploration. What was the music that came out of the fields and churches, the stages and the streets, the marches, the hit parades, and sports fields? We'd need to vary not just their stories but also the emotions of the evening.

I remember at one point, looking up and seeing, suspended from the ceiling, what almost looked like toy airplanes, one seater with a small front propeller. I wasn't at all sure what they were or why they were there, but finding out would lead us to one of the most moving segments of the show.

Our show would be a two-hour entertainment special for ABC, taped at the Kennedy Center on a Saturday night, the last televised event with the Obamas still being President and First Lady. The next morning, we would also produce the opening dedication ceremonies whose speakers included Supreme Court Chief Justice John Roberts Jr., Former President Bush, and President Obama. It was a more formal affair of speeches but did include a big spontaneous hug between President Bush and Michelle Obama, which set the mood of the morning. The whole weekend was one of celebration and honest memory, attended by overflow crowds and a lot of happy faces, who came to see the Museum take its place on the National Mall.

My co-producers, Charlie Haykel and Julianne Hare, and I read and listened to a lot of music, had meetings with curators and Lonnie Bunch. We decided to film some of the items in the Museum to show as projections during a performance, linking the museum artifacts to performances on the Kennedy Center stage. Other treasures in the Museum would be part of short pre-filmed, stand-alone pieces.

Our music director, Rickey Minor, was a key member of our creative team, an unending source of musical ideas. He knew these songs in his blood and shaped their arrangements together with the performers in ways that heightened the emotions of the evening, helping us transform the night into more than just a concert.

Some of the segments we decided on were the birth of the blues, which began with slaves in the field picking cotton singing to blues guitarists, followed by a performance of "Catfish Blues" by bluesman Gary Clarke Jr., followed by the Alvin Ailey dancers, and a thirty-second video narrated by Morgan Freeman, showing a bill of sale for a six-year-old slave girl named Sallie who had "light skin and dark brown eyes" and worked in the fields.

Jada Pinkett Smith told how Marian Anderson sang on the steps of the Lincoln Memorial when the doors of Constitution Hall were closed to her, as we saw images of Anderson's dress in the Museum. Mary J. Blige gave a stirring rendition of "God Bless America," the song Anderson sang, backed by the Howard University Gospel Choir.

Top contemporary singers brought back the signature songs of the great Black women of jazz and popular music, Billie Holiday, Lena Horne, Sarah Vaughan, and Ella Fitzgerald, interspersed with their mementoes in the Museum. Janelle Monáe introduced the music of the '60s, from soul to rock, R&B and songs from the civil rights movement, as we saw sheet music and Chuck Berry's Cadillac, photos, awards and clips from the Museum, followed by musical tributes to Motown, James Brown and Michael Jackson, among others, and sports legends like Muhammed Ali.

John Legend hushed the audience with Marvin Gaye's urgent plea from the civil rights movement, "What's Going On." Common spoke the words of Langston Hughes, Samuel Jackson said jazz had been the sound of freedom and cool throughout the world, before Herbie Hancock came out to play "Watermelon Man."

What we didn't predict was that the sequence that got the longest, loudest ovation and tears featured seven men, all of them over the age of eighty. The unsung heroes who had flown those tiny airplanes in World War II we saw hanging from the ceiling of the Museum—the Tuskegee Airmen.

When we learned about their prolonged fight for the right to fly a plane in battle in the still-segregated armed forces, and the outsized courage they showed in the air, we knew we had to include their story in the show.

To my mind, there is no celebrity who has spoken out with more passion and respect about those who fought in World War II than Tom Hanks. He is associated with it from his movies and mini-series, as well as his many personal appearances and writings over the years. I spoke with Lonnie Bunch about the idea of inviting him, and Lonnie could not have been more encouraging.

When I contacted Tom Hanks, his first response was—well, I can't really say what Tom thought, because there was a long pause. He hesitated to speak and then said he was concerned he might be the wrong person. He wondered how it would seem to have a white actor do this. I was able tell him that Lonnie Bunch was hoping he'd do it. Not because he was white or Black but because he was a serious World War II history buff, and this was a little known but crucial World War II story.

Then Hanks laid out his other concern. Were we willing to be honest about what had really happened; how the doors of segregation were so firmly closed against young Black men who wanted to play a role in the fight? He knew enough already to know some of its ugly truths. Yes, I told him, be honest. Tell the whole story.

I turned to my longtime colleague and writer Sara Lukinson and asked her to prepare a draft of what Hanks might say, giving her my suggestions and directive not to skim over the stories. With the Museum's help, she got in touch with the few surviving airmen, listened to their stories, read whatever had been written about them or by them, and about the military's segregation policies at the time.

Her draft to Tom Hanks began, "In 1941, after Pearl Harbor, millions of young people—the ones we'd later call the greatest generation—signed up to do whatever it took to fight for democracy and freedom. However, if you were an African American who enlisted to help save the world, chances are you'd have to do it as a cook, a truck driver, a grave digger, or by unloading supplies. African Americans may have been fighting in America's armies since the Revolutionary War, but the military remained as segregated as the line to the whites-only drinking fountain. As segregated as major league baseball and the movies." Sara really got it.

She continued, "Young, talented, airplane crazy African American guys were told, 'Combat flying? Taking care of expensive planes? Not for you. You can't handle it.' But that year, a few laws cracked the doors open. Military training programs were set up at Black colleges. President Roosevelt banned discrimination in all defense industries. And the first all-Black Fighter Squadron came into being at the Tuskegee Institute in Alabama. It started with thirteen cadets."

The draft went on, longer than any of our other introductions. It included how the program grew to 1000 men, the 15,000 sorties and bomber escort missions they flew, the 200 German aircraft they shot down. It quoted one airman who spoke of how they all flew for their parents, their race, their country, and for first-class citizenship. He said they shared the sky with white pilots, but never had contact with them afterwards. Despite their heroics, it took almost fifty years for their story to be told, including how their actions helped to end segregation in the military.

Hanks read the draft and agreed immediately. Then we began to build our segment. Seven of the surviving airmen were well enough to attend. As Hanks spoke, we would show images of their planes hanging in the Museum and photos of their young faces, before bringing the men on stage. Then, the West Point Glee Club, in full military choir uniforms would sing, "America the Beautiful."

The weekend of the show, Quincy called Colin Powell, who agreed to come out on stage and salute each of the men and shake each of their hands. When Tom Hanks showed up to rehearse, he brought more thoughts and statistics he wanted to add. We asked him to finish his piece by introducing the seven men with these words, "In 2007, they were finally awarded the Congressional Gold Medal. President Bush said then, as we say tonight, 'For all the unreturned salutes you endured and on behalf of the country that honors you, I salute you.'"

The seven Tuskegee Airmen came onto the stage, some on walkers or in wheelchairs, but with their spirits soaring. Their broad smiles lifted the whole room, and we saw not their age, but their heroics. Hanks—elated by their presence and happiness in being there—burst into a huge grin that never left his face. Colin Powell surprised the airmen when he was introduced by Tom Hanks. He saluted the airmen with admiration and respect, and they saluted back.

When Powell began to shake each of their hands, the audience leapt to their feet, applauding, screaming, and whistling. The ovations, these long overdue thank-yous, went on for a long time, and the more the Tuskegee Airmen beamed and waved back, the more the place erupted, tears streaming down the faces of the audience.

At the end of the show, Stevie Wonder urged everyone there to love one another, before beginning to sing. The entire cast joined him for the rousing finale, including the seven Tuskegee Airmen. Suddenly and spontaneously, the cast ushered the men into the front line and started taking selfies with them, while the men seemed to be dancing on air (and walkers)! Waves of feeling went from the stage to the audience and back again.

History was alive that night. It was filled with tears and laughing, hurts and happiness, reminders, and celebrations. And nowhere was it more alive than in the faces of the seven Tuskegee Airmen, who embraced Tom Hanks as the cheering and singing and crying went on until the evening reluctantly came to an end, and the life of the Museum officially began.

MAKING HISTORY WITH TELEVISION
OBAMA'S INAUGURAL CONCERT AT THE LINCOLN MEMORIAL

It was Sunday January 18th, 2009. Early morning light was just beginning to break in the East as we climbed into our van on 16th Street in Washington DC. It was bitter cold, and seventeen degrees with wind gusts up to thirty miles per hour. We drove across the National Mall, heading for the eastside of the Lincoln Memorial, where our makeshift production camp had been set up. As we passed the Washington Monument, we could see hundreds of families, bundled up in gloves, hats and heavy overcoats, making their way with flashlights to the Reflecting Pool in front of the Lincoln Memorial. Before long, there would be 700,000 people, a sea of smiling faces braving the cold, waiting for the concert, and to be able to say, I was there, I was part of that day in history.

Our Sunday afternoon concert was the first of the celebrations to mark the inauguration of Barack Obama, the young, vibrant, first African American to be elected President of the United States. He was a man who ran on the theme of hope. Everyone wanted to be there, and every performer in the country wanted to be on the show. We had less than six weeks to put it together. I don't know if I slept but I know I felt like my whole life had led me to this moment. To be able to use television to bring the country together, to share the same surge of emotions as it welcomed the promise of a new era.

As a young man, I had seen how television brought the country together in grief after the death of President Kennedy, and now I had the chance to have television bring us together in joy. As it turned out, I'm glad I had a lifetime of television experience, because I was going to need it.

The call to direct and produce the show came from the producer Ricky Kirshner, a friend I had worked with many times. He worked closely with the Democratic National Committee and the Obama organization and would oversee several televised events but wanted to hand over this concert to me, along with co-producer George Stevens Jr., and his son Michael.

Although we started thinking about the show in December, it took a while for Obama's inaugural team to finally decide what they wanted to do and what they could afford. They had limited funds which had to be spread over several events and what they could give us was quite a bit less than a big show like this costs. We didn't know how that would affect things, but we couldn't really know, because we did not get a green light on "We Are One" until eleven days before the event itself. It was crazy. You had to do five things at once and trust that everyone on your team was as dedicated as you were. And they were. We all felt this show was our chance to give something to the country. We felt like the Mission Impossible team.

Since we couldn't wait for the final approval to do a survey, and we'd need that information no matter what the show turned out to be, we paid a crew ourselves to make a full technical survey a few weeks ahead of time. When we finally got the green light, we had our long to-do list ready, which included securing permits, designing, and building a stage with a massive heating system in the floor, and working with the Secret Service to plan the security for the Obamas and the Bidens. We had to erect giant screens and sound towers from the Lincoln Memorial around the Reflecting Pool all the way back to the Washington Monument, a distance that stretched across more than 4,000 feet, equal to the size of a dozen football fields. It was a monumental task (no pun intended).

We also had to book the talent. We had hoped to get a broad range of entertainers from all areas of the country and types of music, and actors to do the introductions and read passages from American history. We wanted to celebrate the election but also celebrate the country itself and place this day in the ongoing story of America. However, given the difficult and rushed conditions, the lack of rehearsal time and space, the bitter cold, and our inability to pay stars what they were used to, or for that matter, pay them at all, or their travel expenses, hotels, meals, or even pick-ups from the airports, we anticipated a lot of no, thank-yous. I began to think of back-up ideas and wonder how we would pull this off. But what happened stunned me.

Not one person we invited blinked an eye. We'll be there, on our own dime. We'll pay for our hotel and get ourselves to the stage. What time do you want me? Within days, we had enough talent for a twenty-hour show. What would we give everyone to do? We'd have to start grouping stars together. I laughed—and cried—to think of how everyone would have to rehearse in canvas tents thrown together with aluminum scaffolding, no walls and a few room heaters. Everyone would have to practice with their hats, scarves, and jackets on. All in the few days and hours before the show.

HBO was going to carry the concert live, which meant they would cover some of the costs. They always charged viewers for these kinds of special events but they agreed to broadcast this concert free to the entire world. The title of our concert was "We Are One" because we felt it fit the mood of the country. Now, it also fit everyone who wanted to be associated with the show.

Hope is not something you can easily define, or can assume will be there, but that day you could feel it everywhere. It lifted everyone's spirits, brought out their generosity and their best selves and a desire to be part of the whole. It floated in the air, like the feeling you have on the first warm day of spring. This concert was being built in eleven days with the best talent in the country, and it was made with pure joy. One look at the audience, wrapped in their coats, hats, scarves, gloves, and boots, clapping, and singing along, you knew they felt it too.

We wanted to open the show with the feel and flourish befitting a new president, and asked the US Army Band and the Herald Trumpets to play Aaron Copland's "Fanfare for the Common Man." Beyoncé, who at first wanted to open the show agreed with me that she'd be stronger as the finale, singing an anthem-like version of "America the Beautiful," backed by a 300-voice choir standing behind her on the steps of the Lincoln Memorial. She sang the song so beautifully, embracing every word and instilling every phrase with meaning, sharing those feelings with the crowd. As she neared the song's end, the entire cast came out to join her on stage and bring the concert to its end, on a note of grace and unity. As Beyoncé came to the very last words, "shining sea," she reached for the highest note, like she was reaching for the sky and flew there on wings of emotion, as if suspended in time. After she finished, she uttered "wow," as if she had surprised herself, and then burst into a huge smile as she spontaneously said to the crowd, "America, we are one."

I was glad I was able to change her mind, because looking back and judging by the soaring emotional response that ending brought, it was one of the best decisions I ever made. It was a glorious moment.

So many people had come for the chance to perform, that we were able to team various artists together to sing with one another, which opened many musical options we may never had had the chance to try. Everyone agreed to our pairings and song choices, another first in my experience. Our ideas were a joint effort between us, our musical director, and the musical director of all the choirs.

Jon Bon Jovi and Bettye LaVette delivered a powerful rendition of Sam Cook's "A Change Is Gonna Come." James Taylor and his wife Kim, John Legend, and Jennifer Nettles sang "Shower the People." Herbie Hancock, Will. i.am, and Sheryl Crow did a jazz infused version of "One Love." Usher, Stevie Wonder and Shakira joined together on "Higher Ground." Bono sang with his U2 band—having paid for them all to come, it was hard to say no.

We were also able to add choirs to many performances, because for me nothing lifts a song higher than the power of many voices raised together in song. We used almost a thousand voices in all, in several choirs. Bruce Springsteen sang "The Rising" with the Joyce Garrett Singers. Then near the end of the show, he joined Pete Seeger and the Inaugural Celebration Chorus for "This Land Is Your Land." Renée Fleming sang "You'll Never Walk Alone" backed by the 150 voices of the US Naval Academy Glee Club. Josh Groban and Heather Headley sang "My Country Tis' of Thee," with the 200 voices of Washington DC's Gay Men's Chorus. And with a rocking Baptist Choir setting the tempo, John Mellencamp delivered "Little Pink Houses."

In between the musical numbers, we had actors read famous passages from American history, and quotes from Presidents and American historical figures. We wanted all of America to be heard that day. Those who read included Denzel Washington, Laura Linney, Ashley Judd, Jaime Foxx, Steve Carell, Marisa Tomei, George Lopez, Jack Black, and Samuel Jackson. Tom Hanks read Aaron Copland's stirring "Lincoln Portrait," as our orchestra played, and images of Lincoln were seen across the screens.

I was directing from the truck and while my mind raced in a thousand directions, I was surprised at how smoothly everything was going. No one malingered on the stage, hogged the spotlight, threw a temper tantrum backstage or got confused as to where to go.

One stage moment I especially remember was when Garth Brooks came out, backed by the Inaugural Celebration Chorus, to sing a medley of "American Pie" by Don McLean, and "Shout" by the Isley Brothers. Garth is so good at getting his audiences revved up, and this audience was so raring to go, that everyone was soon singing—all the words—to "American Pie." Then, Garth launched into "Shout" and every time people heard him say the word, "Shout!" they would say it back and jump up in the air. Now sound travels slowly, so when Garth said, "Shout" the audience closest to him on the stage would jump up and then, a fraction later, the sound rippled down to the crowds, and then they heard, "Shout" and jumped up. It created a human wave of thousands of people spontaneously jumping in the air that ran from the Lincoln Memorial down the Reflecting Pool to the Washington Monument. It took my breath away. I stole a few moments to enjoy it before I had to go back to my director's headset.

The concert was seen around the world. The Associated Press called it, "Near flawless with multiple camera angles and the majestic backdrop of Abraham Lincoln." It was an uplifting, almost spiritual experience for me, all the better because I could share it with my son, Charlie, who was working on the show as a volunteer. The day was gray, bitter cold, and windy, but the concert chased away all of winter's darkness and chill. There was magic in the air for everyone gathered around the Lincoln Memorial, the Reflecting Pool, and the Washington Monument.

I felt proud to be at the helm of such an extraordinary moment, a day that brought out the best of everyone. It wasn't the last show

I produced and directed, but I felt it had brought my years in television full circle, from the time in Austin when I was barely more than volunteer myself—intrigued, infatuated, and awed by the power of television to bring us together at an overwhelming moment in our lives. "We are One" was television at its best, when everyone worked together to let the country share this momentous and joyous day in American history.

EPILOGUE

This has been a collection of stories of what happened when my childhood fascination with the flickering lights of early television met up with my lifelong desire to walk the high wire of event television. In many ways, television and I grew up together.

At first, I was just fascinated with the toys of the trade—the cameras, the lights, and the giant editing machines which back then were as slow as a horse and buggy and kept in rooms so cold we had to wear gloves. As my experiences grew, I began to realize that television was more than just magical wires and machines, it was becoming the storytelling medium of our time. The television screen was now where we gathered to watch and share our days, our experiences, and our emotions. The family and friends who sat in front of a TV screen were being connected by television to their neighbors and the world, especially when we dealt with tragedy or triumph.

The more shows I made, the more I came to understand that I wanted to do more than cover an event, I wanted to be a communicator and storyteller and create my own events. To make every event or program a story I was there to tell, whether with a single performer or thousands of cast members in Olympic Stadiums.

Shows, if I did them well enough, would allow viewers to make discoveries, rapt in surprise, and touched with joy or tears. I wanted to learn how to keep their attention and interest in the story as we unfolded it, to help them appreciate the impact a performance or show might have to connect audiences around the planet, not only to the performers on the stage, but to one another.

What has always been key for me is finding the emotional center of each show and each moment, and how it can be expressed. Every decision I've made, whether it's about where to put a camera, and when to cut away, which songs to suggest, how deep a blue to wash on the stage, when the dancers should enter, or how many times the pyro should go off—it comes from that place. Intensive homework and preparation, then assembling a team of dedicated craftsman is where it starts and goes on without let up until the show is on the air.

Some of the shows I've done have been among the largest spectacles seen on television, while others have been music in a concert hall, or solemn ceremonies for a few hundred people. The size never mattered. In each case you are searching for the beating heart of that show, or that moment, and how to transmit that to those who are watching. So often for me that connection came through music. Music has been a part of me since I played a fender steel guitar in high school, perhaps it's the way I find it easiest to express my own feelings. Music connects us in a deep emotional way, and so it was through the music I loved, and music I learned to love through our different shows, that helped me find ways to reach the audience and help tell the show's story.

I do worry sometimes television specials today are much more style over substance. Trying to impress viewers with flash and glitz rather than trying to touch people's emotions. There are too many directors who mistake making a flashier show for a memorable one. It's never the size of the budget or the production that matters, it's the size of the ideas. Technology has made things work so fast it's become too easy to add more pizazz and special effects that while impressive shortcut your thinking. You think no one will know what's missing, but that is not true. Audiences may not put it into words, but they know when a show hits them in the solar plexus, and tugs at their heart, because that is the show they remember.

Everything about making a show is about the process of getting there. Ideas grow as you work on them; failures make you take a new direction you would never have thought of before. You have to keep your mind from folding in a panic from sudden changes, whether in the weather, belligerent talent, or world events.

As time went on, I was lucky to have a ringside seat at some of our biggest national occasions. As well as smaller and moving ones. I treasure every connection I made with artists who I admired, adored, or just met, and to communicate with them through the music and the dance, the cello, and the songs.

I've worked with great performers, choreographers, writers and designers, as well as some who just acted like they were. I've also worked with presidents, international figures, scientists, and a Shah. Some were easy to work with, while others were curt and distant.

I've had my share of wrong calls, shows I probably should not have done, others I wish I had done better. Every live show is one where you only get one chance to get it right. Award shows sound glamorous but keep you creatively boxed in, and more could go wrong than go right, but they do help you put your kids through school.

Usually, I've worked through knotty problems with patience, but a few times by threatening to quit. I always tried to encourage and show my appreciation to my team, and everyone involved, but regrettably I've also lost my temper. Or feel I've failed.

Looking back over a lifetime of shows and experiences, there is much that I remember with pride. I've had a chance to play a small role in the life of my country through television, hopefully as a storyteller who left a few memories in people's lives.

My life as a director and producer brought me opportunities I never dreamed existed back when I was nine years old sitting with my dad, my mouth open and my mind whirring at the big cameras broadcasting live the Mariachi bands, square dancers, and country singers who performed on a basketball court for San Antonio's first television program.

There aren't enough thank-yous in the world for all the colleagues I've worked with, masters of their craft, creative and technical, who helped take an idea and keep at it until we've made it soar as best we could. All of them willing as I was, to put in the hours to fix one cue, change one color, re-block one band, or fix one edit. Or to cajole, argue and plead on the phone to get us what we felt a show deserved. Every show is a work in progress until it goes out over the air.

A confession. With every show I did, large and small, each time I counted down ten seconds into a live broadcast, I sat there tightly coiled with the combined emotions of a worried father and an astronaut belted into the rocket about to take-off as I thought, "The world is watching, will this even work?"

Nerve wracking, scary, intense, adrenalin-pumping exhilarating. The director's chair is where I lived for sixty years. I loved every thrilling, terrifying moment of it. And miss it to this day.

ACKNOWLEDGMENTS

Anyone who has spent ten minutes in this business knows that everything happens because of a collection and collaboration of people equally dedicated, talented, and committed to highest standards, always willing to go the extra mile to solve the impossible. There is no show or event I've directed or produced that could have happened without the unseen artists, craftsman, business people, music directors, stage managers, electricians, drivers, location managers, and on and on. I wasn't able to mention all of them in this book, so with my apologies and greatest of thanks for making me look so good, (the failures were my own), I want to salute and thank the following people and beg the forgiveness of those whose names I omitted due to my own faulty memory.

First, to my co-author Sara Lukinson, who continually encouraged me. This book would never have been written without her.

To my four children—Charlie, Lilly, Jennifer, and Heather—who challenged my approaches, triggered new ideas, and reminded me of stories long forgotten. To my whole family, who I endlessly burdened with my constant preoccupation in writing this book.

To Alan Reback, who is so much more than my business manager, a man who has a passion for show business and knows how it works inside and out, and most of all is a trusted longtime friend. Alan has walked the walk with me, step-by-step, for decades. To David Goldberg who was by my side in so many of my experiences from the very beginning; George Schlatter, a mentor who believed in me when I thought

I was finished, and my career was over; Sandy Wernick, my agent for decades at the Brillstein Company, who made my deals fairly, but firmly; and Michael Seligman, supervising producer on dozens of shows.

To the University of Texas where my passion for television was triggered and cultivated six decades ago, and to Bob Squier who in 1963, helped me get a grant from the Ford Foundation to take a gap year at the University of Texas, while en route to my PhD, to roll up my sleeves, and work in the Studios of KLRN Channel 9 on the University campus. I painted scenery, pulled cable, hung lights, ran camera, and learned the nuts and bolts of television from the ground up.

To Charles Guggenheim, three-time Oscar winner, who hired me to make films when I was struggling with a new family in Washington DC just after my graduation from college. Guggenheim taught me how to tell stories better by not always obeying the rules.

To my creative partners through the decades: To Kenny Ortega, a director and choreographer who elevates every production he's worked on, Nina Lederman who has joined us on dozens of shows as co-producer; Geoff Bennett, a creative production supervisor who we lost way too soon; Music Directors Rickey Minor, Steve Jordan, Mark Watters, Glen Roven, and Harold Wheeler; Michael Seligman and Danette Herman in Production Supervision and talent; Lighting Designers Bob Dickinson, Noah Mintz, Bob Barnhart, and Bill Klages in the early days; Writers Jon Macks, David Wild, Buz Kohan, Dave Boone, and so many others; Associate Directors Jim Tanker, Gregg Gelfand, Michael Polito, and Jan Cornell; Stage Managers Gary Natoli, Garry Hood, Dency Nelson, Arthur Lewis, and Valdez Flagg, and Production Designers Basil Walter, Steve Bass, Bob Keene, Bruce Rodgers, and Jeremy Railton, among many others.

To Kerry Smith and Daniel Regan, my legal supports, who have helped me to negotiate hundreds of contracts and protected me in areas that I really never fully understood.

To Charlie Haykel and Juliane Hare, my long-time associates who are now partners at Don Mischer Productions. They are carrying the torch forward as my involvement has been winding down. Carry on!

And to my hardworking and loyal executive assistant, Kirsten Judson, for keeping my life and business in some sort of reasonable order. And before Kirsten, my thanks to Ben Roy, Jason Uhrmacher, and Maureen Kelly. These patient people had to deal with my micro-management and constant second guessing. God bless them. I'm sure that many times they thought there must be an easier way to make a living.

Thanks also to Chris Heiser and Tyson Cornell for being the first to read my completed manuscript, and gave me hope that it might get published.

To my family in Texas who accepted my leaving our home state to pursue my career elsewhere. I'm the only Mischer to have left Texas and taken up residence in another state—some Texans would consider that as being a traitor, of course. Thanks, in particular, to my younger sister, Terrye, and my brother, Doug. We have shared and survived our family experiences—the happy times and the gut-wrenching times—for all of our lives. And Terrye and Doug were my cast and crew when filming with my 8mm Bell and Howell camera in the early days in Texas.

And to all the network executives who "green lit" Don Mischer Productions, trusting us with hundreds of shows costing millions of dollars; allowing us to reach people, touch their hearts and give them millions of memories.

Finally, to all the artists who trusted me to help them express their creative visions through the medium of television. Those collaborations were the best part of my job.

INDEX